MEDELLÍN & COLOMBIA'S COFFEE REGION

ANDREW DIER

Contents

MEDELLÍN AND THE COFFEE REGION

Medellín is one of the most dynamic cities of Colombia, with a vibrant cultural scene and nightlife. However, the hallmarks of this region are the coffee plantations and tiny Paisa pueblos. This verdant countryside, with its exuberant vegetation and many shades of green, is simply spectacular.

© ANDREW DIER

HIGHLIGHTS

LOOK FOR ◖ TO FIND RECOMMENDED SIGHTS, ACTIVITIES, DINING, AND LODGING.

Museo de Antioquia
◖ Medellín

Jardín
◖

◖ Reserva Natural
Río Claro

◖ Salamina

Parque
◖ Nacional Natural
Los Nevados

Museo del Oro — ◖ ◖ Valle de Cocora ⊛ BOGOTÁ
Quimbaya

Jardín
Botánico
del Quindío

© AVALON TRAVEL

◖ **Museo de Antioquia:** The galleries of this art museum, a fabulous art deco building from the early 20th century, are filled with works from the best Colombian artists spanning nearly four centuries. And the terrace café is the best place for people-watching in the Centro (page 11).

◖ **Reserva Natural Río Claro:** A jungle paradise in the Magdalena Medio is set along a canyon that was only relatively recently discovered. This private natural reserve offers caving, river rafting, and a surplus of peace (page 32). ·

◖ **Jardín:** Just a few hours south of busy Medellín, the pace of life slows to a crawl in this picture-perfect coffee town of brightly colored Paisa homes. Jardín is surrounded by lush green mountains full of recreational opportunities (page 36).

◖ **Salamina:** Life goes on much as it always has in this rather remote Paisa town known for its superb architecture and warm hospitality of its people (page 52).

◖ **Parque Nacional Natural Los Nevados:** Dozens of hikes leading through tropical jungles afford fantastic views of snowcapped volcanoes and mountain lakes in this easily accessed national park (page 55).

◖ **Museo del Oro Quimbaya:** This fantastic gold museum pays tribute to the original settlers of what is now the fertile coffee region: the indigenous Quimbaya people (page 61).

◖ **Jardín Botánico del Quindío:** This is the best botanical garden in the region. You take a guided tour through a tropical forest full of *guadua* forests and dozens of species of birds. (page 63).

◖ **Valle de Cocora:** One of the most dramatic and photographed scenes in Colombia is this valley filled with towering wax palms, Colombia's national tree. Nearby Salento offers coffee plantations and a typical Paisa pueblo experience (page 69).

Jardín, a town in southern Antioquia

Medellín, the surrounding department of Antioquia, and the coffee region departments of Caldas, Risaralda, and Quindío comprise the central, mountainous section of Colombia, covering the Cordillera Central (Central Range) and Cordillera Occidental (Western Range) north of Cali. The mountains then flatten out into the Caribbean coastal lowlands. Antioquia and the coffee region lie on some of the most beautiful mountain landscapes in Colombia.

HISTORY

Despite its inaccessible terrain, Antioquia was an important province of colonial Nueva Granada due to its abundant gold deposits. It attracted settlers who panned the rivers or cultivated food for the mining camps. Santa Fe de Antioquia, founded in 1541, was the main colonial settlement.

After independence, the province continued to prosper, even attracting foreign investment in gold mining. Demographic pressure triggered a southward migration known as the *colonización*

antioqueña. Waves of settlement brought Paisa families to unoccupied lands in the south of Antioquia, the coffee region, and the northern part of the Valle del Cauca.

During the early part of the 20th century, coffee was a major source of prosperity in Antioquia. Medellín grew rapidly and became the industrial powerhouse of Colombia. The last decades of the 20th century were difficult times for Antioquia, with the triple scourge of drug trafficking, paramilitary armies, and guerrillas. In the past decade, the government has made huge strides in bringing back the rule of law, and today Antioquia is one of the safest and most prosperous regions in Colombia.

PLANNING YOUR TIME

Weather-wise, anytime of the year is a good time to visit Medellín and the coffee region. There's a reason why they call Medellín the "City of Eternal Spring": The entire region has a temperate climate.

Medellín completely empties during the end of

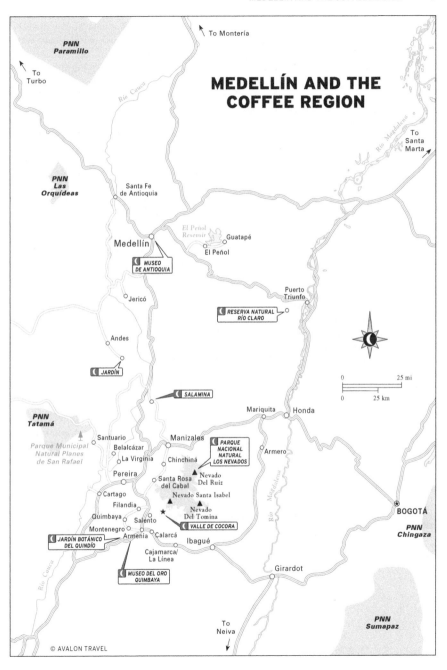

MEDELLÍN AND THE COFFEE REGION

the year holidays, from December 15 to January 15, and also during Semana Santa (Easter week). This is peak time for pueblos and coffee region haciendas. During school vacations (June-July), natural parks and reserves and coffee haciendas get busy again.

Give Medellín three days. During that amount of time, you can experience "old Medellín" sights in the Centro, such as the Museo de Antioquia, as well as check out the modern Medellín icons that are the subject of great pride: the Metrocable, Biblioteca España, the café culture of cool El Poblado, and the Parque Explora. Consider spending a weekend in Medellín, when hotel rates drop, and especially if you're interested in checking out the city's nightlife scene. In a week you can add one or two other destinations in Antioquia, such as the Reserva Natural Río Claro or one of the picture-perfect Paisa pueblos, such as Jardín or Jericó. These are within about a three-hour bus ride from the Antioquian capital of Medellín.

Many visitors visit the gorgeous colonial town of Santa Fe de Antioquia to the north of Medellín as a day trip, but it's better to spend one night there, in order to enjoy strolling its quaint streets after the sun has gone down. On the banks of the mighty Río Cauca, Santa Fe is one of the hottest towns in the region. Guatape, with its famous rock, El Peñol, makes for a nice overnight on the way to or back from the Río Claro reserve, where two nights are necessary. These three destinations are popular on weekends and holidays. The stunning natural beauty of Río Claro is best enjoyed during the week.

To the south of Medellín are two picture-perfect Paisa pueblos: Jardín and Jericó. A couple of days in one of those should be enough. You can continue from there southward into the coffee region on winding country roads.

Medellín is not a base for visiting the coffee region: The cities of Armenia, Manizales, and Pereira are. Pereira has good air connections, while the Manizales airport is often shrouded in fog.

One of the joys of this region is to book a few days at a coffee hacienda. Many tour operators will pack your days with day-trip activities. Resist! As it gets dark at 6pm every day, it would be a shame to miss spending some daylight hours strolling the grounds of the *finca* (farm), lazing in a hammock or rocking chair, or doing nothing at all.

You'll need a week or more to decompress on the coffee farm and see the region's top sights: the Valle de Cocora, the Jardín Botánico del Quindío, and Museo del Oro Quimbaya near Armenia, and one or two of the national and regional parks. There are very good transportation links between the three major cities and Salento. Roads are generally excellent. While renting a car in Colombia is not often the best option, here it makes sense.

Though you can enjoy this magnificent region just by taking a bus ride from one place to the next, there are a few spots that warrant special attention. East of Medellín toward the Río Magdalena lays the Reserva Natural Río Claro, a lush, deep canyon. The Parque Nacional Natural Los Nevados and surrounding regional parks (such as Parque Regional Natural Ucumarí) offer innumerable opportunities for day hikes and longer treks. A bit off the beaten track, Parque Municipal Natural Planes de San Rafael offers beautiful hikes in the less-visited Cordillera Occidental.

Medellín

While Medellín is the country's second in terms of population and importance, perpetually behind Bogotá, this city of around 2.7 million is the only Colombian metropolis with an urban train system. It's the first city with a cable car transportation system.

The first settlement in the region, near the present-day Poblado sector, was established in 1616. Medellín proper was founded in 1675, and was designated the capital of Antioquia in 1826.

In the 1980s, Pablo Escobar, born in nearby Rionegro, established a cocaine-trafficking empire based Medellín. In its heyday, the Medellín Cartel controlled 80 percent of the world's cocaine trade. When President Virgilio Barco cracked down on the cartel in the late 1980s, Escobar declared war on the government. He assassinated judges and political leaders, set off car bombs to intimidate public opinion, and paid a bounty for every policeman that was murdered in Medellín—a total of 657. In 1991, Medellín had a homicide rate of 380 per 100,000 inhabitants, the highest such rate on record anywhere in the world. In 1993, Escobar was killed while on the run from the law.

During the 1990s, leftist guerrillas gained strength in the poor *comunas,* or sectors, of Medellín, waging a vicious turf war with paramilitaries. At the turn of the century, the homicide rate was 160 per 100,000 inhabitants, making Medellín still one of the most dangerous places on Earth.

Shortly after assuming power in 2002, President Álvaro Uribe launched Operación Orion to wrest the poor *comunas* of Medellín from the leftist guerrillas, and violence decreased notably. By 2005, homicides were still high by international standards but a fraction of what they had been a decade before. Under the leadership of Mayor Sergio Fajardo, elected in 2004, and his successors Alonso Salazar and Aníbal Gaviria, Medellín has undergone an extraordinary transformation. In partnership with the private sector, the city has invested heavily in public works, including a new cable car transportation system, museums, and libraries. In recent years, the city has become a major tourist destination and has attracted significant foreign investment.

Medellín boasts a network of spectacular public libraries, greenspaces and plazas, and its train and cable car system. Beyond the Centro, the neighborhood of Laureles and the municipality of Envigado have their own distinct identity and atmosphere.

Orientation

Medellín is in the Valle de Aburrá, with the trickling and polluted Río Medellín dividing the city into east and west. Both the Metro (Line A) and the Avenida Regional or Autopista Sur, a busy expressway, run parallel to the river.

The main neighborhoods are El Poblado, including the mini-hood of Provenza, the Centro, and the Carabobo Norte area (often referred to as Universidades).

The El Poblado area is full of great restaurants, bars, hostels, hotels, and glitzy shopping malls. It is also full of tall brick high-rise apartment buildings, home to the well-to-do. If you arrive in Medellín from the Rionegro airport, you will descend the hill into the valley and land more or less in El Poblado. Luxury hotels and malls line the Avenida El Poblado. The Parque Lleras is the center of the Provenza neighborhood, a small, leafy, and very hip part of El Poblado. It is on the eastern side of the Avenida El Poblado. To the west, down the Calle 10, is the Parque del Poblado, and a few blocks farther is the El Poblado Metro station.

Across the river from El Poblado is the Terminal del Sur bus station and the Aeropuerto Olaya Herrera. The Cerro Nutibara (Pueblito Paisa) is north of the airport. Northwest of the Cerro Nutibara is the quiet neighborhood of Laureles, and farther west is the stadium area. The B line of the Metro connects the Centro with the stadium area.

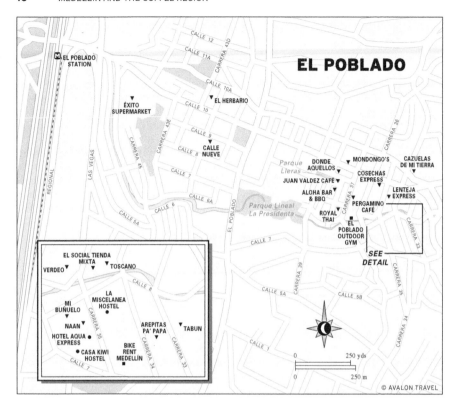

Between El Poblado and the Centro is the Barrio Colombia and an industrial area known appropriately enough as Industriales. This is an up-and-coming area with new hotels and high-rises being built in what is known as the Ciudad del Río, where the Museo de Arte Moderno de Medellín is located. Barrio Colombia is also home to many nightspots.

The heart of the Centro is the Plaza Botero and Parque Berrío Metro station area. The Centro is between El Poblado to the south and Carabobo Norte to the north. The Avenida El Poblado, also known as Carrera 43A, connects El Poblado with El Centro. The Metro does as well.

The northern neighborhoods of Medellín are massive. To the west of the Río Medellín there are few places of interest. The Cerro Volador is a hill and landmark in the northwest of the city. To the east of the river is the Aranjuez neighborhood. The Acevedo Metro station is where you can pick up the Metrocable to the Biblioteca España and Parque Arví.

On the other side of town, in the far south, are the municipalities of Envigado and Itagüi. Envigado has some great restaurants, a busy main plaza, and the Parque El Salado. The Avenida El Poblado connects El Poblado with Envigado. Itagüi is an industrial town with little of interest for the tourist except for bars and clubs, many open until the wee hours.

Safety

As in other cities in Colombia, it is best to avoid hailing taxis on the street, particularly at night. Instead, have your hotel, or the restaurant or shop you're at, call a taxi for you. Be careful at clubs and bars, and don't accept drinks from strangers.

Neighborhoods such as La Provenza and Laureles are safe to walk about day or night. The Centro should be avoided after dark. It is not a good idea to take a carefree stroll in the northern or western neighborhoods or, especially, in the *comunas* (city sectors) on the surrounding hills, but specific sights mentioned can be visited. Not only are they clean and efficient, but the Metro, Metrocable, and Metroplús are safe.

SIGHTS

To see Medellín in full motion, visit the Centro during the week. On Saturdays, it's quieter, although the Peatonal Carabobo bustles with activity. On Sundays downtown is almost deserted except for tourists and street people. Most visits to the Centro start from the Parque Berrío Metro station. The main sights can easily be seen on foot and in a few hours.

Centro

◖ MUSEO DE ANTIOQUIA

The Museo de Antioquia (Cra. 52 No. 52-43, tel. 4/251-3636, www.museoantioquia.org.co, 10am-5:30pm Mon.-Sat., 10am-4:30pm Sun., COP$10,000) is one of the top art museums in the country, with an extensive permanent collection of works from Colombian artists from the 19th century to modern times. Look for the iconic painting *Horizontes* (*Horizons*) by Francisco A. Cano. It's a painting that depicts the *colonización antioqueña,* when, for a variety of reasons, families from Antioquia headed south to settle in what is now known as the coffee region. In the contemporary art rooms, you'll see *Horizontes* (1997) by Carlos Uribe. This painting presents the same bucolic scene, except this time, 84 years later, in the background, a plane is seen spraying pesticides over the countryside, in an attempt to kill coca and marijuana crops. Native son Fernando Botero has donated several of his works, over 100 of them, to the museum. There is also a small room on a series of works by Luis Caballero. The

museum is in an architectural gem, an art deco-style building from the 1930s. It originally served as the Palacio Municipal. There is a free guided tour at 2pm every day.

Carabobo Norte

One of the country's top universities is the Universidad de Antioquia (Cl. 67 No. 53-108, tel. 4/263-0011, www.udea.edu.co). The university was founded in 1803; however, it has only been at its current location in the Ciudad Universitaria, a few blocks west of the Centro, since 1968. There are over 37,000 students enrolled here, and the campus, full of plazas and public art, has a vibrant student energy In addition to a busy calendar of cultural events, the university has an excellent museum, MUA (Cl. 67 No. 53-108, Bloque 15, tel. 4/219-5180, www.udea.edu.co, 8am-5:45pm Mon.-Fri., 9am-12:45pm Sat., free), that features changing contemporary art exhibits and a permanent natural history exhibit. Access to the campus for all visitors is at the Portería del Ferrocarril entrance. Visitors must present a photo ID.

Adjacent to the university near the Metro station, the Parque Explora (Cra. 52 No. 73-75, tel. 4/516-8300, www.parqueexplora.org, 8:30am-5:30pm Tues.-Fri., 10am-6:30pm Sat.-Sun, COP$18,000) is one of the most iconic buildings of modern Medellín. It's a series of four futuristic red boxes. The ticket office closes 90 minutes before closing time. The aquarium (9am-5pm Tues.-Fri., included in admission cost) is the highlight of Explora. This is one of the largest aquariums in Latin America. Check out the tanks of Colombian marine creatures, including life in Colombian rivers such as the Amazon and Orinoco. Look for the giant pirarucú, an endangered fish that lives in the Amazon River and in its tributaries. The Planetario Medellín (Cra. 52 No. 71-117, tel. 4/516-8300, www.planetariomedellin.org, 8am-5pm Tues.-Wed., 8am-7pm Thurs.-Fri., 10am-6pm Sat.-Sun., COP$12,000) is across the street from the Parque Explora.

If you feel like a walk in the park, the Jardín Botánico de Medellín (Cra. 52 No. 73-298, tel.

4/444-5500, www.jbmed.org, 9am-5pm daily, free) is the place for you. It is across the street from Parque Explora. The highlight here is the Orquiderama, an open-air wood lattice-like structure where events are held. The botanical gardens are more akin to a tropical city park. It's a popular hangout for students, who will giggle as they say hello to you in English. In addition to the fantastic setting and good food of In Situ (inside the gardens, tel. 4/460-7007, www.botanicomedellin.org, noon-3pm Mon., noon-3pm and 7pm-10pm Tues.-Sat., COP$25,000), there are cafés and a nice gift shop.

Behind the botanical gardens is the Esquina de las Mujeres (Cra. 51 at Cl. 73), a small public space with busts of accomplished women from Medellín and Antioquia from the colonial era to the present day. They represent many walks of life: indigenous women, activists, social workers, and artists who all made a contribution to society. Not many locals know about this homage, which was unveiled in 2007.

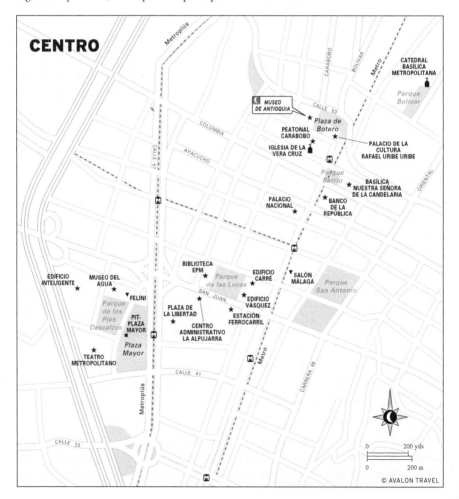

Presidents, artists, and writers rest in the Museo Cementerio de San Pedro (Cra. 51 No. 68-68, tel. 4/516-7650, www.cementeriosanpedro.org.co, 8am-5:30pm daily, free). Marble statues and elaborate tombs pay tribute to influential Antioqueños from the 19th century onward, but the reminders of the city's recent turbulent past may strike you as more interesting. One plot, near the tomb of Fidel Cano, founder of the once influential *El Espectador* newspaper, contains the tombs of several members of drug kingpin Pablo Escobar's associates and guards. (He is buried in a cemetery in the neighboring town of Itagüi.) Some tombs have stickers identifying allegiance to one of Medellín's soccer clubs, others have touching handwritten notes from wives and children left behind. There is a free tour of the cemetery on Sundays (2pm). To see the cemetery in a different light, check it out on a full moon evening (7pm-9pm). It's open to the public then and there are usually free concerts and other cultural activities going on. Check the cemetery's up-to-date webpage for a complete schedule of activities.

Cerro Nutibara

To see an authentic Paisa pueblo, go to Jardín, Jericó, or Salamina. They're just a couple of hours away and are as real as you can get. Can't do that? Then go to the Pueblito Paisa (Cl. 30A No. 55-64, tel. 4/235-6476, 5am-midnight daily, free), atop the Cerro de Nutibara, one of two hills that interrupt the flat landscape of the Valle de Aburrí. Here, at this rather cheesy celebration of Paisa culture, you'll be greeted by smiling folks decked out in traditional costume. There is also a small Museo de la Ciudad. Plenty of food and handicrafts are on sale here. Also on the hill are a sculpture park and an amphitheater. You could go just for the views: From this high point there's a good view of Colombia's second city. The hill is also a popular place for an early morning jog. The Pueblito Paisa is lit with thousands of multicolored lights at Christmastime.

Northern Medellín

The Casa Gardeliana (Cra. 45 No. 76-50, tel. 4/213-5965, Barrio Manrique, 9am-5pm Mon.-Sat. 10am-4pm Sun., free) has wall-to-wall tango memorabilia and some cool souvenirs. Plus a seat from the ill-fated airplane that crashed in the city and killed tango icon Carlos Gardel. Unfortunately, the museum does not tell the story of tango in Medellín in a clear manner, but it is just steps from the Metroplús Manrique station. If you are visiting downtown or the Cementerio de San Pedro, from there you can easily hitch a ride on the Metroplús.

In the neighboring barrio of Aranjuez is the Casa Museo Pedro Nel Gómez (Cra. 51B No. 85-24, Barrio Aranjuez, tel. 4/233-2633, free). This delightful museum houses an extensive collection of the painter's works, including several murals for which he is best known. Much of his work portrays the plight of campesinos (rural peasants), workers, and indigenous people. His house, now the museum, was designed by Gómez, and the location of it was chosen by his Italian-born wife. The hills overlooking the city here reminded her of Florence, somehow. In the new wing of the museum there is a small public library. The courtyard holds a snack bar-café. The museum is not easy to get to, and you will probably have to take a cab there. Many visitors combine this visit with a trip to the nearby Casa Gardeliana.

BIBLIOTECA ESPAÑA

When this public library was opened in the low-income neighborhood of Santo Domingo, King Juan Carlos came from Madrid for the ceremony. Spain, after all, helped to fund the project. It's one of many newly created *biblioteca parques* (public library parks) in Medellín. More than a place for books, these library parks have become community centers and sources of pride in neighborhoods that continue to struggle with poverty and violence. The Biblioteca España (Cra. 33B No.107A-100, tel. 4/385-7531, www.reddebibliotecas.org, 8am-7pm Mon.-Sat. and 11am-5pm Sun.) is the most famous and most visited of the 24 public libraries in the city, and,

Downtown Medellín Walking Tour

PLAZA BOTERO TO THE PLAZA DE LOS PIES DESCALZOS

Medellín's brash downtown is a compact history tour comprising stoic remnants from the colonial era, brick and mortar evidence of Medellín's rising as Colombia's most important industrial center in the early 20th century, and the vibrant public spaces, modern transportation systems, and futuristic architecture showing this proud city's 21st-century optimism.

Begin the tour at the Parque Berrío Metro station and walk five minutes north to the Plaza Botero.

PLAZA BOTERO

Most visits downtown begin under the shadows of the Palacio de la Cultura Rafael Uribe Uribe (Cra. 51 No. 52-03, 8am-5pm Mon.-Fri., 8am-2pm Sat., free), an occasional host of art exhibits. The Plaza Botero (in front of the Museo de Antioquia, Cra. 52 No. 52-43) gets its name for its 23 corpulent bronze sculptures by Fernando Botero. Passersby often pose in front of the sculptures, such as La Mano (The Hand) and Eva (Eve) for a quick snapshot. One of the most prolific, and by far the best known, of contemporary Colombian artists, Botero donated these sculptures to his hometown of Medellín. His paintings and sculptures of rotund people often portray campesino (rural) life, but many of them are also commentaries on the violence in Colombia.

PEATONAL CARABOBO

To the south, the Peatonal Carabobo is a pedestrian walkway that extends for eight blocks. Lined with shoe shops, five-and-dime stores, and snack bars, it's busy, loud, and colorful. (Although there is usually a police presence, be sure to watch your stuff!)

On the right-hand side is Medellín's oldest church, the brilliantly white Iglesia de la Vera Cruz (Cl. 51 No. 52-38, tel. 4/512-5095), which dates back to 1682. It is often filled with working-class faithful, sitting or standing in meditation and prayer. It's a refuge of quiet in this busy commercial area. The only other living testament to Spanish rule in Medellín is the white-washed Basílica Nuestra Señora de la Candelaria on the Parque Berrío a few blocks away.

The Belgian architect who designed the grandiose Palacio Nacional (Cra. 52 No. 48-45, tel. 4/513-4422) in the 1920s probably never expected that it would, over time, become the domain of around 400 tennis shoes and jeans vendors. It was originally built to house governmental offices, and today, when you walk through the corridors of this historic building, all you'll hear is the chorus of "a la orden" ("at your service!") from hopeful shop attendants. Towards the end of Peatonal Carabobo is Donde Ramón, a small kiosk in the middle of the walkway, jam-packed with antique objects like brass horse stirrups or old carrieles (leather handbags) from Jericó.

PARQUE DE LAS LUCES

After years of abandonment and urban decay, in 2005 the artificial forest of the Parque de

like each of them, it is stunning. The library resembles giant boulders clinging to the edge of the mountainside. It was designed by architect and Barranquilla native Giancarlo Mazzanti, who won a prize for this work at the VI Bienal Iberoamericana de Arquitectura y Urbanismo in Lisbon in 2008.

Getting to Santo Domingo is an attraction in itself. The neighborhood is connected to the metropolis by the Metrocable cable car system.

Take the Metro towards Niquía station and transfer to the Metrocable at Acevedo. The Santo Domingo station is the third and final stop.

When the Metrocable K line was opened in 2004, it was the first of its kind in the world: a gondola-like public transport system with a socio-economic purpose, connected to a metro. The system, consisting of gondolas, has eliminated eternal climbs up and down the mountain for low-income residents.

las Luces or Plaza Cisneros (Cl. 44 at Cra. 52) was opened in an effort to rejuvenate the area. The park, consisting of 300 illuminated posts, looks somewhat odd during the day but is spectacular at night when it shines. Check it out by car at night as it is not safe to roam about after dark. On the east side of the plaza are two historic early-20th-century brick buildings: the Edificio Carré and Edificio Vásquez (Cl. 44B No. 52-17, tel. 4/514-8200). When they were built they were the tallest buildings in Medellín. These buildings were once important warehouse facilities during the industrial boom of the early 20th century. The plaza used to be the home of the main marketplace. On the western side of the plaza is the Biblioteca EPM (Cra. 54 No. 44-48, tel. 4/380-7516, 8:30am-5:30pm Mon.-Sat.), a stunning public library sponsored by the electric company EPM (Empresas Públicas de Medellín), built in 2005. In addition to reading rooms, there are occasional exhibitions and cultural events held at the library.

Across from the Parque de las Luces on the southern side of Calle 44 is the Estación Ferrocarril (Cra. 52 No. 43-31, tel. 4/381-0733), the old main train station. There's not much to see here, except for a train engine and forgotten old tracks.

PLAZA MAYOR

To the west of the Estación Ferrocarril is the Centro Administrativo La Alpujarra (Cl. 44 No. 52-165), which houses the Departamento de An-tioquia government offices. The sculpture Homenaje a la Raza, by Rodrigo Arenas Betancur, stands in the middle of the large intermediary plaza. Just beyond is the Plaza de la Libertad (Cra. 55 between Clls. 42-44), a complex of modern office space and interesting public space complete with urban gardens.

Cross the pedestrian bridge over the lanes of the Metroplús bus station. Metroplús is the latest addition to Medellín's transportation network. It debuted in 2013. Here is the Plaza Mayor (Cl. 41 No. 55-80, www.plazamayor.com.co), the city's preeminent convention and event venue; it has a fair share of nice restaurants. The Teatro Metropolitano (Cl. 41 No. 57-30, tel. 4/232-2858, www.teatrometropolitano.com), built from 20th-century brick, hosts concerts.

Finally, the Plaza de los Pies Descalzos (Cra. 58 No. 42-125) is a plaza filled with a *guadua* (Colombian bamboo) forest and fountains, where you can take off your shoes and play. It's surrounded by eateries on one side and the massive Museo del Agua (Cra. 57 No. 42-139, tel. 4/380-6954, 8am-6pm Tues.-Fri., 10am-7pm Sat.-Sun., COP$4,000) on the other. In the distance is a long-standing Medellín architectural icon: the Edificio Inteligente (Cra. 58 No. 42-125, tel. 4/380-4411). Built in the late 1950s, it has served as the headquarters of EPM, the utility company. To find out what's so smart about it, you can take a free tour of the building. They are offered Monday-Friday. Call in advance to reserve.

PARQUE ARVÍ

For some fresh, and oftentimes crisp, country air, a visit to the Parque Arví (Santa Elena, tel. 4/444-2979, www.parquearvi.org, 9am-5pm Tues.-Sun., free), covering 16,000 hectares (40,000 acres) of nature, hits the spot after a few days of urban exploring.

Highlights in the park include the seven well-marked nature paths, which meander through cloud forests thick with pine and eucalyptus trees, over brooks, along ancient indigenous paths, to mountain lakes and lookout points with spectacular views of the Valle de Aburra and Medellín below. Most paths, with a distance of under three kilometers (two miles), are not strenuous whatsoever. There is a longer path of over 10 kilometers (six miles) that is excellent for biking. Ask at the information booth upon arrival at the Arví Metrocable station for

Getting Up the Hill

During the late 1990s to 2000s, thousands of families from rural areas in Antioquia, Córdoba, and Chocó were forced to leave their homes due to violence. Moving to Medellín to start a new life, many arrived in the low-income neighborhoods along the steep slopes of the mountains surrounding the city. But here, where many live in meager brick homes covered with corrugated zinc roofs secured only by large stones, horrific violence has followed them. First it was turf wars between guerrillas and paramilitaries in the early 2000s. Today the violence is caused by drug-trafficking gangs with links to former paramilitaries. This wave of violence has given birth to a new phenomenon: intra-urban displacement, during which families have been displaced within the city due to urban violence. For many, this is the second displacement that their families have had to endure.

City leaders have sought to improve the quality of life in the *comunas* in a variety of innovative ways. Two lines of the Metrocable gondola system have made a huge difference in allowing residents to travel to work or school in the city without having to walk up and down the mountainside. Spectacular modern public libraries have been built in many low-income communities, providing a safe and pleasant space to study, read, and connect to the Internet. These have developed into important cultural centers, with an active schedule of films, children's activities, and other cultural activities. New homes have been built and donated to 200-300 displaced families in the neighborhood, with funds from the national government under President Juan Manuel Santos.

In 2012, the city debuted its latest project, this time aimed at improving life in the Comuna 13, the most notorious of the *comunas* in the entire city. This time the project involved the creation of open-air escalators in this neighborhood. These are a series of six dual, interconnected escalators that extend down the slopes for some 384 meters (1,260 feet). The system operates from early in the morning until about 10 at night. They are monitored by city employees, and their use is free. It is the first time in the world escalators have been used in order to improve the lives of the less fortunate.

The escalators have made a difference in the lives of Comuna 13 residents, although there are some who believe that the money spent on the project (around US$6 million) could have been better used otherwise. There have been alarming reports as well that some gangs have been intimidating residents by charging them to use the escalators, under the threat of dire consequences.

Despite the high levels of violence affecting residents (never foreign tourists), the escalators have become a tourist attraction, and even appear in the city's tourism promotional materials. Celebrities and dignitaries from President Juan Manuel Santos to French fashion designer Francois Girbaud have taken a ride on the escalators.

It is indeed a strange kind of tourism, with which some may feel uncomfortable. However, if you would like to see this escalator project, you certainly can. Go during the day, and you must not wander the streets of the Comuna 13. Never remain in the neighborhood after dark. To get there, take the Metro Línea B to San Javier station. As you depart the station, in front are *colectivos* (small buses) that regularly transport passengers to the Comuna 13. It's about a 15-minute trip and costs under COP$1,500. Ask anyone which bus to take, and let the bus driver know that you'd like to go to the *escaleras eléctricas.*

From San Javier, there is also a Metrocable line (Línea J) that has three stops and travels to the top at La Aurora.

A trip to the Parque Arví in northern Medellín is an excellent break from the city.

suggestions on walks to make. There are often free guided nature walks as well.

Other recreational activities are on offer in the different *nucleos* (nuclei) of the park. Understanding the nuclei and layout of the park can be confusing. Staff at the information booth at the entrance will provide you with a map and assist you in planning your visit. At the Nucleo Comfenalco, you can rent a paddleboat on the Piedras Blancas reservoir, and there is a small hotel, as well as a butterfly pavilion. In the Nucleo Mazo there is a market.

To explore the park on bike, you can rent a bike for free with the city's Encicla program by showing an ID card. These can be rented at any of the several Encicla stations in the park, but you will be required to renew the rental at any station if you have been cycling for more than an hour. Encicla staff can provide you with a map and recommendations.

The park is a nice day trip to make, and you might consider the getting there the best part about the excursion. To get there from the city, take the Metro to the Acevedo station in the north of the city (Línea A towards Niquía). From there, transfer to the Metrocable (Línea K) to the Santo Domingo station. From there you must transfer to the Parque Arví line (Línea L, COP$4,200 one way), which has an additional cost.

The temperature can drop substantially and abruptly in the park. Pack along a light sweater and a lightweight rainproof jacket. Try to get an early start so that you can enjoy the park without rushing. There are various snack bars and restaurants throughout the park.

Southern Medellín

The Ciudad del Río area, between downtown and El Poblado near a Metro line, has developed into an up-and-coming neighborhood largely due to the arrival of the Museo de Arte Moderno de Medellín (MAMM, Cra. 44 No. 19A-100, tel. 4/444-2622, www.elmamm.org, 9am-5:30pm Tues.-Fri., 10am-5:30pm Sat., 10am-5pm Sun., COP$8,000). The coolest part about the MAMM is its location in an old warehouse, typical of the Barrio Colombia area. This was the home of Talleres Robledo, a steel mill that began operations in the 1930s. Exhibitions (usually two at a time) are hit or miss. The museum store, the *tienda,* is an excellent place to pick up a whimsical Medellín souvenir. Many items, like T-shirts, notepads, or cute doo-dads, are the product of local creative minds.

The Parque El Salado (Vereda El Vallano, Envigado, tel. 4/270-3132, www.parqueelsalado. gov.co, 9am-5pm Tues.-Sun., COP$3,000), a municipal park covering 17 hectares (42 acres) in Envigado, has trails and activities, such as a zipline, and is a good place to get some fresh air. On weekends it gets packed with families on a *paseo de olla.* Literally a soup-pot excursion, *paseo de olla* usually means *sancocho,* a hearty beef stew. Essential gear for a day out at the park includes giant aluminum pots for slowly heating a *sancocho* over a campfire. There is plenty of fresh air at this park, but from afar it may appear that there is a forest fire in the picnic area with all of the campfires. Getting to the park is easy using public transportation. From the Envigado Metro station look for a green bus with a sign that says Parque El Salado. It's about a 20-minute ride up towards the mountains.

ENTERTAINMENT AND EVENTS
Nightlife

Since 1969, El Social Tienda Mixta (Cra. 35 No. 8A-8, tel. 4/311-5567) has been selling the basics to local residents (soap, sugar, coffee); it's only been a recent phenomenon that it's now the hippest place to be seen at night, when it is converted into the most popular bar in Provenza! It's so popular on weekend evenings, you can forget about finding a vacant plastic chair.

Want to check out the nightlife with other party people? That's the idea behind the Pub Crawl Medellín (cell tel. 300/764-6145, pubcrawlmed@gmail.com, Sat. evenings, COP$30,000). In this night of shenanigans, revelers (groups of about 12) get together, then hit several bars (enjoying courtesy shots along the

way), and then wind up the night dancing to the beats at a popular dance club. Each Saturday the group explores different nightspots.

Every Thursday evening, the Medellín microbrewery 3 Cordilleras (Cl. 30 No. 44-176, tel. 4/444-2337, www.3cordilleras.com, 5:30pm-9pm Thurs., COP$20,000) offers a tour of their brewery, during which you learn about the beer-making process. At the end of the tour, the grand finale is tasting several of their artisan beers and friendly socializing. On the final Thursday of each month, after the tour there is live music and beer.

Calle Nueve (Cl. 9 No. 43B-75, tel. 4/266-4852, 6pm-2am Mon.-Sat., no cover), in a nondescript white house, is a hipster's paradise in El Poblado. Music varies wildly from salsa to house to folk. The dim lighting and well-worn couches provide the perfect chilled-out atmosphere.

SALSA, TANGO, AND JAZZ

Medellín is no Cali, but salsa has its aficionados here. If the musical genres *son, la charanga, el guaguanco,* and *la timba* don't mean anything to you now, they might after a night at Son Havana (Cra. 73 No. 44-56, tel. 4/412-9644, www.sonhavana. com, 8pm-3am Wed.-Sat., cover Sat. COP$8,000) often has live performances. Nearby is El Tíbiri (Cra. 70 at Cl. 44B, hours vary Wed.-Sat.), an underground salsa joint on Carrera 70, which is hugely popular on the weekends. They say the walls sweat here, as after 10pm it gets packed with revelers, many of whom are university students. Friday nights are big at El Tíbiri.

The downtown Salón Málaga (Cra. 51 No. 45-80, tel. 4/231-2658, www.salonmalaga.com, 9am-11pm daily, no cover)—boy, has it got character. It's filled with old jukeboxes and memorabilia, and has its clientele who come in for a *tinto* (coffee) or beer during the day. The Saturday tango show at 5:30pm and oldies event on Sunday afternoons are especially popular with locals and travelers alike, but a stop here is a fine idea anytime.

Near the Parque de la Periodista, a major weekend hangout for the grungy set, there are some small bars big on personality. Tuesday nights are bordering on legendary at Eslabón Prendido (Cl. 53 No. 42-55, tel. 4/239-3400, 3pm-11pm Tues.-Sat., cover varies), a hole-in-the-wall salsa place that really packs them in! El Acontista (Cl. 53 No. 43-81, tel. 4/512-3052, noon-10pm Mon.-Thurs., noon-midnight Fri.-Sat.) is an excellent jazz club downtown. It's got a bookstore on the second floor and live music on Monday and Saturday evenings. They've got great food, too, making it an excellent stop after a day visiting the Centro.

An authentic tango spot in Envigado is Bar Atlenal (Cl. 38 Sur No. 37-3, tel. 4/276-5971, 3pm-2am daily). Friday night is the best time to go to see a tango performance, but to listen to some tango music from the juke box and have a beer, go any day of the week. It's an institution, with more than six decades of history. Allegiance to the soccer club Atlético Nacional is evident on the walls of the bar. Included is an homage to star player Andrés Escobar. Also in Envigado is La Venta de Dulcinea Café Cultural (Cl. 35 Sur No. 43-36, tel. 4/276-0208, www.laventadedulcinea.jimdo.com, 2pm-11pm Mon.-Sat.), where salsa, *milonga,* and tango nights are often held. Check the webpage for a schedule.

DANCE CLUBS

Famous Mango's (Cra. 42 No. 67A-151, tel. 4/277-6123, 5pm-6am daily, no cover), decked out like a Wild West saloon, is a festive club popular with foreigners and locals alike, and gets going late. Jesús Dulce Mío—Mil Juguetes (Cra. 38 No. 19-255, Km. 2 Vía Las Palmas, tel. 4/266-6020, www.fondadulcejesusmio.com, 7pm-3am Tues.-Sat., COP$10,000 cover) is a popular club near El Poblado. Wednesday is karaoke night.

If you go to Fahrenheit (Cra. 42 No. 79-125, Itagüi, tel. 4/354-6203 www.discotecafahrenheit. com, 10pm-6am Thurs.-Sat., cover varies) you should dress to impress. It's a late-night place in the neighboring town of Itagüi. Thursdays are electronica nights, while Saturdays are for crossover, a mix of popular music with Latin tunes. Guys should expect to pay around COP$25,000 for cover, ladies *nada.*

GAY BARS AND CLUBS

There is a lively gay and youthful nightlife scene in Medellín. Donde Aquellos (Cra. 38 No. 9A-26, tel. 4/312-2041, cell tel. 313/624-1485, 4:30pm-2am daily) is an easy-going kind of place near the Parque Lleras in El Poblado. This friendly bar is a good place for a terrace drink. Culture Club (Cra. 43F No. 18-158, hours vary Thurs.-Sat., cover varies) is the hottest dance club and gets hopping at around midnight on weekends. It's a fashionable place, with chandeliers and red velvet.

Cinema and Theaters

Otraparte (Cra. 43A No. 27A Sur-11, tel. 4/448-2404, www.otraparte.org, 8am-8pm Mon.-Fri., 9am-5pm Sat.-Sun.) is a cultural center that offers a dynamic program of free concerts, films, book launches, and even free yoga classes in Envigado.

Festivals and Events

Festicamara (www.festicamara.com), an international chamber music festival, is held in March or April each year, with concerts across the city at venues like the fabulous Orquiderama in the Jardín Botánico.

The Festival Internacional de Tango (www. festivaldetangomedellin.com) takes place each year during the last week of June, commemorating the anniversary of the death of Carlos Gardel. This festival, and in fact the perseverance of tango culture in Medellín, is largely due to one man's passion and efforts. Argentine Leonardo Nieto visited Medellín in the 1960s, primarily to get to know this city where tango icon Carlos Gardel died in an airplane crash. He fell in love with the city, stayed, and created the Casa Gardelina and the Festival Internacional de Tango. During this festival, tango concerts and events take place across the city, in nightclubs, theaters, parks, and on street blocks.

Since 1991, Medellín has hosted an impressive Festival Internacional de Poesía de Medellín (www.festivaldepoesiademedellin.org), which routinely attracts poets from dozens of countries, who share their work in more than 100 venues across the city. It's held in early July.

International Day of Laziness

Paisas are known throughout Colombia to be some of the most hard-working and driven people in the country. The Medellín Metro, routine 7am business meetings, the orderly pueblos in the Antioquian countryside, and even former president Álvaro Uribe, a native Paisa, are examples of this industriousness. Uribe's famous words upon taking office in 2002 were *"trabajar, trabajar, trabajar"* ("work, work, work"). Laziness is quiet simply anathema to Paisas. But you can't be productive *all* the time. The people of Itagüi, an industrial town bordering Medellín, have taken that to heart. In fact, on one day each year they not only take it easy, they embrace and celebrate the virtues of slothfulness during their Día Internacional de la Pereza (International Day of Laziness) celebrations. On that day in August, residents rise at the leisurely hour of 10am, put out their hammocks and beds in front of their houses, and laze the day away, sometimes still in their pajamas. The day's events include a bed (on wheels) race and general goofing off. Ironically, most of the action (or inaction) of that day takes place in the Itagüi Parque del Obrero (Worker's Park).

As the leading textile manufacturing center in Colombia, Medellín is the obvious choice for the most important fashion event in the country: Colombiamoda (http://colombiamoda. inexmoda.org.co). It attracts designers and fashionistas from across the globe, and during this week, the Plaza Mayor becomes a fabulous model-fest.

The Feria de las Flores (www.feriadelasfloresmedellin.gov.co) is the most important festival of the year in Medellín, and is when the city is at its most colorful. It's a week-long celebration of Paisa culture, with horseback parades, concerts, and the highlight, the Desfile de los Silleteros. That is when flower farmers from Santa Elena show off incredibly elaborate flower arrangements in a parade through the city streets. The festival takes place in July or August each year, and it's a great time to visit the city.

At Christmastime, Medellín sparkles with light, every night. It all begins at midnight on December 1, during the Alborada. That's when the sights and sounds of fireworks and firecrackers envelop the entire Valle de Aburrá. On December 7, the Alumbrado Navideño, the city's Christmas light display, begins. The Cerro de Nutibara and the Río Medellín, along with other city sites, are illuminated with 14.5 million multi-colored lights. Sponsored by the electric company, it's an incredible sight to behold.

SPORTS AND RECREATION
Biking

The Medellín Ciclovía (8am-1pm Sun.) has many routes, including along the Avenida El Poblado and along the Río Medellín. On Tuesday and Thursday evenings there is a Ciclovía Nocturna (8pm-10pm) on two routes: along the river and around the stadium area. Not to be outdone by their neighbor, the cities of Envigado and Itagüi also have a Ciclovía on Sundays.

Encicla (office in Éxito Colombia store, Cl. 48D No. 66-61, tel. 4/436-6271, cell tel. 310/390-9314, 8am-6pm daily, www.encicla.gov.co) is Medellín's bike share program. It's free to use for those over the age of 18. Nice routes are along the Carrera 70 and around the universities. Visitors must register in person at the Encicla office, and must show their passport. Encicla bike paths follow Carreras 65 and 70, connecting with the Estadio and Universidad Metro stations. In Parque Arví (Santa Elena, www.parquearvi.org) there are six Encicla en el Parque stations. At this park, the registration procedure is less involved.

Bike Rent (Cra. 35 No. 7-14, cell tel. 310/448-3731, www.bikerent.com.co, 9am-7pm Mon., Wed., and Fri.-Sat., 9am-10pm Tues. and Thurs., 8am-1pm

Sun., COP$25,000 half day, COP$35,000 full day) rents good bikes cheaply, and the prices decrease as the number of hours you rent them increases. They also have information on routes and suggestions at this convenient Provenza location.

Ciclo Barranquero (tel. 4/538-0699, cell tel. 314/806-5892, ciclobarranquero@gmail.com, COP$70,000-90,000 pp) organizes interesting day-trip bike rides for all levels of cyclists in the city and beyond, such as in the nearby pueblo of Santa Elena and in Guatape. Bikes and necessary equipment are included in the price, but transportation to the meeting point is not. Ecoturismo Arewaro (Cra. 72A No. 30A-21, tel. 4/444-2573, cell tel. 300/652-4327, www.ecoturismoarewaro.com, COP$46,000 pp) organizes day-trip walks and bike trips in parks and pueblos near Medellín. *Arewaro* means "gathering of friends" in the Wayúu language.

Yoga and Gyms

Atman Yoga (Tr. 37 No. 72-84, tel. 4/311-1132, www.atman-yoga.org, donations requested) holds free yoga classes every day at its main location in Laureles. They are quite popular, especially in the evenings. There are also classes at the Jardín Botánico on Tuesdays and Thursdays at 5:30pm and at other times during the week. In El Poblado there are several yoga studios, such as 108 Yoga (Cl. 5 Sur No. 30-72, tel. 4/266-7232) and Sati Yoga Y Meditación (Cl. 10 No. 36-14, 2nd floor, tel. 4/352-4143, cell tel. 315/499-6625).

The gym El Molino (Cra. 79 No. 37-55, tel. 4/411-2714, 5am-10pm Mon.-Thurs., 5am-8pm Fri., 8am-3pm Sat., 9am-2pm Sun., COP$35,000 weekly pass) in Laureles has a large weight room, cardio machines, and a pool and sauna, and holds various classes. You may not think of schlepping all the way to Envigado to get in a workout, but at multi-level Dinamo Fitness (Tr. 29S No. 32B-126, tel. 4/334-1512, www.dinamofitness.com, 5am-10pm Mon.-Thurs., 5am-2pm Sat., 8am-2pm Sun.) the price is right. A two-day pass costs COP$22,000, a ticket for six entries is COP$60,000, and a ticket for 12 entries is COP$120,000.

Many parks in Medellín have outdoor gyms where you can get in a free workout. These are especially popular with young men who work out on the *barras* (pull-up bars). One such gym is in the Provenza barrio (Cra. 37 at Cl. 8); another is in the Ciudad del Río behind the Museo de Arte Moderno de Medellín (Cl. 20 at Cra. 45).

Paragliding

For incredible views of both the verdant Antioquian countryside and the metropolis in the distance, check out a paragliding adventure organized by the Aeroclub San Felix (Km. 6 Vía San Pedro de los Milagros, tel. 4/388-1077, www.parapenteencolombia.com, 20-min. flight COP$80,000, complete course COP$1,600,000). Bus transportation to the town of San Felix is available from the Portal del Norte bus station, and the Aeroclub San Felix can also arrange transportation from El Poblado for an additional cost.

Centro Deportivo Atanasio Girardot

At the Centro Deportivo Atanasio Girardot (Cras. 70-74 and Clls. 48-50, tel. 4/369-9000, pool tel. 4/430-1330, ext. 146), in addition to soccer matches and the occasional big-name concert, there are running tracks, basketball courts, and swimming pools free of charge and open to the public, including visitors. To use the pools all you need is to present an ID and bring a bathing cap. They sell them on-site for under COP$20,000. The Olympic-sized pool is only open to those with a membership in the swimming league, but there are four others available to the public. The nice blue track is often packed with Paisas getting in their morning sweat. It's open to the public during the morning hours, and usually on Tuesdays and Thursday evenings it is also open 8pm-10pm. There are also jazzercise, yoga, rumba, and aerobics classes given several times a day starting at 6am. Just show up and join the fun. Call (tel. 4/369-9000, ext. 118) for class schedule information. The complex is accessible from the Estadio Metro station.

the Estadio Atanasio Girardot complex

Soccer

Medellín has two professional teams, and Envigado has one. By far the most famous team, with followers across the country, is Atlítico Nacional (www.atlnacional.com.co). Nacional, wearing the green and white of the Antioquian flag, has been playing since 1947. It's one of the most successful teams in Colombia and has won the top division 11 times. Nacional defeated Santa Fe from Bogotá for the 2013 Liga Postobón championship, which was a very big deal. Nacional is wildly popular with young men and boys in Medellín, Antioquia, and beyond. The cheap seats at Nacional games are always packed with kids from the barrios. The other team in town is Deportivo Independiente Medellín (www.dalerojo.net). This is the oldest club in Colombia and was originally called Medellín Foot Ball Club when it was established in 1913. Their colors are red and blue. Both teams play at the Estadio Atanasio Girardot (Cl. 48 No. 73-10, www.inder.gov.co). Tickets can be purchased at Ticket Factory Express (tel. 4/444-4446, www.ticketexpress.com.co).

Tours

Turibus (www.turibuscolombia.com, 9am-7:40pm daily, COP$28,000 24-hour pass) operates a hopon, hop-off service that has seven stops in the city, including the Plaza Botero and the Cerro Nutibara/Pueblito Paisa. They also offer tours to other parts of the Antioquia department, such as to Jericó and Guatape.

While some may find it unseemly to go on a tour of Pablo Escobar's Medellín, others find it fascinating. During the three-hour Pablo Escobar Tour (cell tel. 317/489-2629, www.paisaroad.com, 10am daily, COP$35,000) offered by Paisa Road, you'll see where the world's most notorious drug baron grew up, learn about the violent world of the cartels, and visit his tomb. The meeting point for the tours (offered in English) is at the Black Sheep and Casa Kiwi hostels in the Provenza area of El Poblado. If you'd like to visit Escobar's grave independently, you can take the Metro to the Sabaneta station. The Parque Jardines Montesacro (Cra. 42 No. 25-51, Autopista Sur Itagüi, tel. 4/374-1111, 9am-5pm daily, free) is within walking distance from there.

SHOPPING

The Provenza neighborhood and the area around Parque Lleras are home to several boutique clothing and accessories shops. Santa Fe (Cl. 43 No. 7 Sur-107, www.centrocomercialsantafe.com) is the largest and flashiest of Medellín's malls. It's on the Avenida El Poblado.

ACCOMMODATIONS

Accommodation options to fit every budget and taste are plentiful in Medellín. El Poblado has the most options, with luxury hotels along the Avenida El Poblado and hostels and boutiques in the walkable Provenza area, close to a smorgasbord of restaurants and bars and close-ish to the El Poblado Metro station. Laureles is a quiet and green residential area with a growing number of fine options for those wanting an escape from the madding crowd. There aren't many reasons anyone would want to stay in the Centro, an area of town that feels unsafe at night. As is the case in cities in the interior of the country, on weekends Medellín empties somewhat, hotel prices fall, and vacancies increase.

Under COP$70,000

Dozens of hostels cater to more than the traditional twenty-something backpacker. Today these economical options offer comfortable private rooms for those who are looking for a friendly environment and keeping an eye on their expenses.

The Casa Kiwi (Cra. 36 No. 7-10, tel. 4/268-2668, www.casakiwihostel.com, COP$20,000 dorm, COP$60,000 d) is a backpacker's institution in El Poblado. A cold and *über*-cool atmosphere pervades the place at times, though, and it does have the reputation of being a party pad (loud). It's got a capacity of 60, with an array of private rooms and dorm options, plus a nice sundeck above. Nonguests can visit on Friday evenings, when there's live music on the deck.

With just one dorm room and two private rooms (with a shared bath), La Miscelanea Hostel (Cra. 35 No. 7-86, tel. 4/311-8635, www.lamiscelanea.co, COP$20,000 pp) is a low-key and relaxed option run by a friendly Paisa couple. This hostel in Provenza started as a restaurant/bar, and they still have occasional live music performances in their bar area. There's lots of vegetarian fare on offer, and it's open to the public. The *tienda* (store) has funky things made by Medellín's creative folk.

 Urban Buddha (Circular 73A No. 38-55, tel. 4/413-9322, www.buddhahostel.com, COP$20,000 dorm, COP$60,000 d) is a friendly place to stay in the leafy neighborhood of Laureles. The garden out back is a peaceful urban refuge and nice place to study one's Spanish or chat with other world travelers. The Spanish owners of this hostel also run the Secret Buddha Hostel (Cl. 94 B Sur No. 51-121, La Estrella, tel. 4/279-5152, cell tel. 312/892-6521, www.buddhahostel.com, COP$25,000 dorm, COP$65,000 d) in the Estrella municipality, outside of Medellín. It's green and quiet out there, but you can still head into town easily on the Metro.

COP$70,000-200,000

In contrast to many Colombian cities, Medellín has a fair variety of midrange hotels. Chain hotels tend to be best, holding few surprises.

The Casa Hotel Asturias Medellín (Circular 4 No. 73-124, tel. 4/260-2872, COP$89,000 d) is on a delightful corner of the tree-lined and quiet Laureles neighborhood. That's the big selling point for this small hotel. Rooms are modern and comfortable, although not terribly huge. It's a good deal.

Well located in the Provenza neighborhood, Acqua Hotel Express (Cra. 35 No. 7-47, tel. 4/448-0482, cell tel. 320/788-4424, www.hotelacqua.com, COP$131,000 d) is a good value. Its 43 rooms are spic and span and comfortable.

French budget chain Hotel Ibis (Cl. 20 No. 44-16, tel.4/444-1554, www.ibis.com, COP$99,000 d) has modern rooms with comfortable beds at great rates, and is located in an interesting area in the Ciudad del Río, across the street from the Museo de Arte Moderno de Medellín. There's no gym, but the neighborhood is quiet, making it a decent place for a morning jog. The best views are on the hotel's south side. The hotel restaurant offers buffet meals for an additional price. On the weekends it's very quiet, and room rates drop to an unbelievable COP$79,000.

Located across from the Atanasio Girardot sports complex, the Hotel Tryp Medellín (Cl. 50 No. 70-24, tel. 4/604-0686, www.tryphotels. com, COP$146,000 d) has 140 large, comfortable (if spartan) rooms and an excellent rooftop terrace with a whirlpool and steam room. Guests have access to an extremely loud gym on the lobby floor. Restaurants are nonexistent in this area, except for street food, and hotel room service is iffy.

The Hotel BH El Poblado (Cra. 43 No. 9 Sur 35, tel. 4/604-3534, www.bhhoteles.com, COP$170,000 d) is across from the enormous Centro Comercial Santa Fe. This Colombian chain hotel with 70 rooms has huge, comfortable beds and modern rooms, and despite its location on a major street (Av. El Poblado), it's not that noisy. An included breakfast buffet is served in a pleasant open-air terrace. It's also got the world's tiniest hotel gym with about three cardio machines.

It's got a boring and frankly ugly location, but the standard-to-the-core GHL Comfort Hotel San Diego (Cl. 31, No. 43-90, www.ghlhoteles. com, COP$124,000 d) offers good prices and the staff is attentive. A mediocre breakfast is served on the top-floor terrace (featuring an excellent view), and amenities include a sauna and small gym. It's close to a couple of malls and is between the Centro and El Poblado on a main road. The Ciclovía passes by in front on Sundays, making it a snap to get out and move.

Hard-core city people will be the ones interested in staying in the Centro. The Hotel Nutibara Conference Center (Cl. 52A No. 50-46, tel. 4/511-5111, www.hotelnutibara.com, COP$132,000 d) is the best choice. It's a faded, grand old hotel located steps from the Museo de Antioquia. With wide corridors and huge rooms with parquet floors, it retains mid-20th-century elegance and personality.

FOOD

The revitalization and resurgence of Medellín that began in the early 2000s has also led to culinary revolution, with countless new dining options popping up throughout the city. The best neighborhoods for dining are Provenza and El Poblado and the Zona M in Envigado.

Colombian

Mondongo's (Cra. 70 No. C3-43, tel. 4/411-3434, www.mondongos.com.co, 11:30am-9:30pm daily, COP$20,000) is a well-known and popular place for typical Colombian food and for drinks with friends. *Mondongo* is a tripe stew, a Colombian comfort food, In addition to the Carrera 70 location there is another Mondongo's on the busy Calle 10 in El Poblado (Cl. 10 No. 38-38, tel. 4/312-2346) that is a popular drinking hole as well. They've even got a location in Miami.

Another popular place on the Carrera 70 strip is La Tienda (Cra. 70 Circular 3-28, tel. 4/260-6783, 10am-2am daily). It's a festive restaurant that morphs into a late-night drinking place as Medellín evenings wear on. Their *bandeja paisa* is famous. It's a signature Antioquian dish that includes beans, rice, sausages, and pork rinds.

Along the Avenida Las Palmas above El Poblado are several large and famous grilled meat and *comida típica* restaurants. They are especially popular on weekend afternoons. Hato Viejo (Cl. 16 No. 28-60, Av. Las Plamas, tel. 4/268-5412 or 4/268-6811, noon-11pm daily, COP$25,000) is a popular place for a weekend lunch with the gang. On Friday nights they have live music. San Carbón (Cl. 15A No. 30-80, tel. 4/311-7602, www. sancarbon.com.co, noon-10pm weekdays, noon-2am on weekends, COP$29,000) often has live music Wednesday-Sunday. Specialties include barbecue pork ribs and pepper steak.

The Provenza area has a number of cute and original Colombian specialty restaurants. Cazuelas de Mi Tierra (Cra. 37 No. 8A-116, tel.

4/448-6810, www.cazuelasdemitierra.com, 8am-5pm Mon.-Wed., 8am-7pm Thurs.-Sat., 10am-4pm Sun., COP$20,000) has a special each day and always plenty of hangover-combating creamy *cazuelas* (stews).

Mi Buñuelo (Cl. 8 No. 35-33, tel. 4/311-5370, 6:30am-8pm Mon.-Sat., 6:30am-3pm Sun.), meanwhile, is a tribute to those unassuming, perfectly round, fried balls of dough, *buñuelos.* Arepitas Pa' Papa (Cra. 34 No. 7-73, tel. 4/352-2455, 11am-2:30pm and 6pm-10pm Mon.-Sat., COP$15,000) lets you create an arepa (cornmeal cake) with your favorite toppings.

Queareparaenamorarte (tel. 4/542-0011, cell tel. 316/741-4458, 12:30pm-8:30pm Mon.-Wed., 12:30pm-10:30pm Thurs.-Sat., 12:30pm-7pm Sun., COP$25,000) is not your typical *comida típica* restaurant. Juilian, owner, chef, and expert on Colombian cuisine, has traveled the country over and has brought the secrets back from grandmothers' kitchens from the Amazon to Santa Marta.

Fusion

In Situ (Jardín Botánico, tel. 4/460-7007, www.botanicomedellin.org, noon-3pm Mon., noon-3pm and 7pm-10pm Tues.-Sat., noon-4pm Sun., COP$30,000) may have the nicest view of any eatery in Medellín. It's surrounded by a million shades of green on the grounds of the Jardín Botánico. It's an elegant place for a lunch, but if you've been sweating it visiting the city, you may feel out of place among the sharply dressed business and society crowds. In Situ has an interesting menu with items such as apple sea bass (COP$30,000) and beef medallions in a coffee sauce with a plantain puree (COP$29,000).

Next to the Museo de Arte Moderno de Medellín is hip Bonuar (Cra. 44 No. 19A-100, tel. 4/235 3577, www.bonuar.com, 10am-7pm Tues.-Fri., 11am-6pm Sat., noon-4pm Sun. holidays, COP$22,000), where the burgers (including a Portobello and lentil version) are famous, but so is the brunch. It's a cool place with a nice outdoor seating area. During weekdays go in the evening when it's livelier.

A classic, old-school restaurant is La Provincia (Cl. 4 Sur No. 43A-179, tel. 4/311-9630, www.restaurantelaprovincia.com, noon-3pm and 7pm-midnight Mon.-Sat., COP$28,000). It is a fusion of Mediterranean cuisine (lots of seafood) with Colombian flair. Reserve a table on the romantic patio out back if you can. Try the exotic grilled fish fillet in a peanut sauce with green papaya strips.

El Herbario (Cra. 43D No. 10-30, tel. 4/311-2537, www.elherbario.com, noon-3pm and 7pm-11pm daily, COP$24,000) has an inventive menu with items such as lemongrass tuna, turmeric prawns, and artichoke risotto. Spacious and minimalistic, it can feel a little like eating in a warehouse, though. The attached store sells exotic jams and chutneys and the like.

American

Chef Ricardo Ramírez studied culinary arts in New Orleans, came back to Colombia, and immediately went to work designing the menu for the Cajun restaurant Stella (Cra. 44A No. 30 Sur-7, tel. 4/448-4640, 11am-11pm Tues.-Sat., 11am-3pm Sun., COP$22,000). He's got things right—there are po'boys, muffaletta sandwiches, catfish, jambalaya, and even alligator sausage. (They get the alligators from a farm near Montería.) The non-reptile crowd can try the vegetarian étouffée. Sunday brunches are often accompanied by live jazz music.

The most innovative restaurant to come Medellín's way in a long time is Aloha Bar & BBQ (Cra. 37A No. 8A-70, tel. 4/444-1148, 11am-11pm Mon.-Thurs., 11am-4am Fri.-Sat., 10am-9pm Sun., COP$25,000). Run by a Hawaiian couple, this is the place for pork sliders, teriyaki ribs, and cole slaw. It's open way late on the weekends, great for a late night nosh after hitting the Parque Lleras bars.

Spanish

Cozy and chic Spanish restaurant El Barral (Cl. 30 Sur No. 43A-38, tel. 4/276-1212, noon-10pm Mon.-Sat., COP$30,000) specializes in paella, tapas, and sangria, and does them well.

Steak

With Colombian newspapers plastered on the walls displaying headlines of yesteryear, the Argentinian steakhouse Lucio Carbón y Vino (Cra. 44A No. 30 Sur-40, Envigado, tel. 4/334-4003, noon-midnight Mon.-Sat., COP$32,000) specializes in grilled steak, paired with a nice Malbec.

British

Cockers Greasy Spoon (Cl. 7 No. 35-56, Provenza, cell tel. 301/520-2668, 9am-2:30pm Tues.-Sat.) knows how to fry up an authentic British breakfast, like baked beans and bacon on toast. They make their own sausage, as well as most everything else on the menu, but the blokes who run the place admit that they don't lay the eggs. For lunch, try the fish and chips. It's a house specialty.

Thai

Authentic Asian restaurants are few and far between. Royal Thai (Cra. 8A No. 37A-05, tel. 4/354-2843, www.royalthaicolombia.com, COP$27,000) gets mixed reviews, and it's expensive, but hey, it's Thai.

Indian

Naan (Cra. 35 No. 7-75, tel. 4/312-6285, COP$22,000) is a small and trendy Indian place in the Provenza area.

Middle Eastern

There are a few good Lebanese and Arab food options in El Poblado and in Laureles. At Tabun (Cra. 33 No. 7-99, tel. 4/311-8209, www.eltabun.com, noon-10pm Mon.-Thurs., noon-11pm Fri.-Sat., noon-9pm Sun., COP$22,000), in addition to usual Arab fare, they also have a few Indian dishes. Plus belly dancers on weekends!

Fenicia (Cra. 73 No. C2-41, Av. Jardín, tel. 4/413-8566, www.feniciacomidaarabe.com, noon-8pm Mon. Thurs., noon-9pm Fri.-Sat., noon-4pm Sun., COP$15,000) is an authentic Lebanese restaurant run by a family who immigrated to Colombia years ago.

Italian

At Crispino (Circular 1A No. 74-04, Laureles, tel. 4/413-3266, noon-11pm Mon.-Thurs., noon-midnight Fri.-Sat., noon-5pm Sun., COP$20,000), owner Salvatore, direct from Naples, offers authentic Italian cuisine.

Whereas most restaurants in El Poblado face rather busy and noisy streets, Toscano (Cl. 8A No. 34-20, tel. 4/311-3094, cell tel. 314/739-6316, 10:30am-11pm Tues.-Sun., COP$13,000 lunch set menu, COP$20,000) is on a quiet street largely isolated from the neighboring riffraff. It's a delight to sit outside and have a pasta dish with a glass of wine.

Vegetarian

Most restaurants except the hard-core Colombian parilla-type places now offer at least one lonely vegetarian dish on their menu. No need to pity the herbivore any longer. In Provenza, make a beeline for the cool atmosphere and fantastic vegetarian food at two-story ◖ Verdeo (Cra. 35 No. 8A-3, tel. 4/444-0934, www.ricoverdeo.com, noon-10pm Mon.-Wed., noon-11pm Thurs.-Sat., noon-4pm Sun., COP$18,000). This vegetarian haven discreetly set at the end of a street in the Provenza neighborhood could be the best vegetarian restaurant in Colombia. Veggie burgers go down well with an artisanal beer, but there are also Asian and Italian inspired à la carte options. Lunch menus are inventive, and are a bargain. Downstairs is more atmospheric, but if you dine upstairs, you can look out over an urban guadua (bamboo) forest. An organic market, Ceres (Cra. 35 No. 8A-3, www.ceresmercadoorganico.com) is on the second floor of Verdeo.

Lenteja Express (Cra. 35 No. 8A-76, tel. 4/311-0186, cell tel. 310/879-9136, 11am-9pm Mon.-Sat.) specializes in veggie burgers: chickpea burgers, lentil burgers, Mexican burgers.

In the Laureles area, Pan y Vida Café (Cra. 51D No. 67-30 Policlinica, tel. 4/583-8386, 7am-7pm Mon.-Wed., 7am-10pm Thurs.-Fri., 7am-4pm Sat., COP$12,000) serves healthy meals, often featuring the Andean super grain quinoa and organic vegetables. At lunchtime they offer a choice of two set meals. Outdoor seating is a fine idea on a pretty day. Pan y Vida is open in the mornings for coffee, juices, and pastries.

Cafés and Quick Bites

Fellini (Plaza Mayor, Cl. 41 No. 55-80, Local 105, tel. 4/444-5064, www.fellini.com.co, noon-8pm Mon.-Fri., noon-4pm Sat., COP$15,000) specializes in burgers, but they also serve sandwiches, salads, and pastas. Plan to eat here after your long day of sightseeing downtown.

The Juan Valdez Café (Cra. 37A No. 8A-74, 10am-9pm daily), atop the Parque Lleras, is a point of reference for the area and the place to meet up with someone for a cappuccino. It's popular with travelers and locals alike.

If you're feeling decadent, as in you'd like your latte in an actual coffee cup and served to you at a table, try Pergamino Café (Cra. 37 No. 8A-37, tel. 4/268-6444, 10am-9pm Mon.-Fri., 11am-9pm Sat). It's on a quietish street in the Provenza area.

Manzzino (Circular 72 No. 38-44, tel. 4/580-7000, 10am-9pm Mon.-Sat., 10am-6pm Sun.) will quickly become your fave Uruguayan neighborhood bakery café in all of Medellín, hands down. They've got apple pies, scrumptious almond cakes, quiches, and sandwiches, and you can enjoy them on a delightful terrace as you watch neighborhood folks go about their business in *tranquilo* (peaceful) and delightful Laureles.

Four in the morning and you've got the munchies? Join the legion of taxi drivers, college kids, and miscellaneous night owls at Trigo Laurel (Circula 1A No. 70-06, tel. 4/250-4943, 24 hours daily). It never closes, not on New Year's not on the 20 de Julio, when Colombians celebrate their independence. They specialize in baked goods, but they also serve cheap lunches. It's on a quiet corner of Carrera 70.

Fresh juices are the specialty at Cosechas Express (Cl. 10 No. 35-25, tel. 4/266-9139, 8am-6:30pm Mon.-Fri., 9am-4pm Sat.). There's an infinite number of possibilities here, as you can mix and match.

INFORMATION AND SERVICES

Spanish-Language Courses

Universidad EAFIT Centro de Idiomas (Cra. 49 No. 7S-50, Edificio 31, Oficina 201, tel. 4/261-9500, ext. 9439 or ext. 9669, COP$880,000 38-hr. course) offers intensive (20 hours per week) and semi-intensive (10 hours per week) Spanish classes. Their courses are certified by the Spanish Cervantes Institute. The Universidad de Antioquia (Cra. 52 No. 50-13, Edificio Suramericana, tel. 4/219-8332, ext. 9003, www.idiomasudea.net) offers personal language instruction at a price of COP$40,000 per hour. Group classes can also be arranged.

A language exchange called "The Lab" takes place every Wednesday at Buena Vista Bar (Cra. 37 No. 8A-83, cell tel. 313/788-7440, 7pm-1:30am Wed.). At this friendly gathering of Colombians, travelers, and expats, you can mingle with others and brush up on (or show off) your Spanish, Portuguese, French, Italian, German, or English skills. Afterwards, enjoy an international fiesta featuring salsa music on the bottom floor and international beats on the upstairs terrace of this cool space in the Parque Lleras area.

Tourist Information

Medellín produces the most comprehensive tourist information of any city in Colombia. In addition to tourist information booths at the bus terminals and airports, there is a large office at the Plaza Mayor (Cl. 41 No. 55-80, tel. 4/261-7277, 8am-noon and 2pm-6pm Mon.-Sat.). The tourism office webpage (www.medellin.travel) is up to date with information on what's going on in the city.

The main newspaper in Medellín is *El Colombiano* (www.elcolombiano.com). Other online resources for events and activities in Medellín and in the area are Medellín Living (www.medellinliving.com), a blog site run by expats; Medellín Style (www.medellinstyle.com), which has information on DJ events in town; Plan B (www.planb.com.co); ticket outlet Tu Boleta (www.tuboleta.com); and Guia Gay Colombia (www.guiagaycolombia.com), for information on gay and lesbian nightlife.

GETTING THERE AND AROUND

It's a snap getting to centrally located Medellín from just about anywhere in Colombia, and from Florida. And once in the Antioquian capital, getting around is pretty easy, too.

By Air

There are nonstop flights from Medellín's Aeropuerto Internacional José María Córdova (MDE, Rionegro, tel. 4/402-5110 or 4/562-2885) to all major cities in Colombia. The airport is simply referred to as "Rionegro." Avianca, LAN, and Viva Colombia operate domestic flights. Internationally, Avianca serves Miami, Panama City, Lima, and Madrid; American Airlines has a nonstop flight to Miami; Spirit and JetBlue to Fort Lauderdale; AeroGal and LAN to Quito; Copa to Caracas and Panama City; and Insel Air to Curaçao.

The Rionegro airport is about 45 minutes (35 km/22 miles) from downtown, depending on traffic. Taxis cost around COP$60,000 between the city and the airport.

Alternatively, there are busetas, small buses, that leave the airport bound for the San Diego neighborhood, which is convenient to El Poblado. These can be found as you exit the terminal towards the right. Upon arrival in Medellín, there are taxis on standby. An organized and legitimate group of young people will help place your bags in the cab, even though you may not want or need this service. They expect a COP$1,000-2,000 tip.

Traveling to the airport, there are buses (Conbuses, tel. 4/231-9681) that depart from a side street just behind the Hotel Nutibara (Cl. 52A No. 50-46, tel. 4/511-5111) in the Centro. These depart from about 4:30am until 7:20pm every day, and the trip costs COP$8,000. The buses are hard to miss: They're green and white

with the word aeropuerto printed in all caps on the front window.

Aeropuerto Olaya Herrera (AOH, Cra. 65A No. 13-157, tel. 4/403-6781, www.aeropuertoolayaherrera.gov.co) is the super-convenient in-town airport. EasyFly serves Montería, Cúcuta, Bucaramanga, Apartadó, and Quibdó; Satena serves Bogotá, Quibdó, Apartadó, Bahía Solano, and Nuqui. ADA (Aerolíneas Antioqueñas) serves a whole slew of cities throughout Colombia, especially western Colombia. The Olaya Herrera terminal was built in the 1930s and is an architectural gem.

Intercity Buses

Medellín has two bus terminals: the Sur and the Norte. The Terminal del Sur (Cra. 65 No. 8B-91, tel. 4/444-8020 or 4/361-1186) is across from the Aeropuerto Olaya Herrera, and it serves destinations in southern Antioquia and the coffee region. The Terminal del Norte (Cra. 64C No. 78-580, tel. 4/444-8020 or 4/230-9595) is connected to the Caribe Metro station. It serves Santa Fe de Antioquia and Guatape, the Caribbean Coast, and Bogotá.

Metro

Medellín's Metro (tel. 4/444-9598, www.metrodemedellin.gov.co) is the only urban train system in the country. It's a safe and super-clean system of two lines: Línea A, which runs from Niquía (north) to La Estrella (south), and Línea B, from San Antonio in the Centro west to San Javier. The Metro line A is useful for traveling between El Centro, El Poblado, and Envigado. Metro line B has a stop at the stadium. The current Metro fare is COP$1,800; however if you think you may use the Metro, Metrocable, and Metroplús system on a regular basis, consider purchasing a refillable Tarjeta Cívica card that is valid on all three transportation networks. The cost per ride with the Tarjeta Cívica modestly drops to COP$1,600. The card can be purchased at Metro ticket booths.

© ANDREW DIER

the Medellín Metro

Metrocable

The Metrocable public transportation system, consisting of gondola *(teleférico)* lines, was inaugurated in 2004 and consists of three lines, with two under construction. It has been internationally lauded as an innovative approach to solving the particular transportation needs of the isolated and poor *comunas* (residential sectors), built on mountainsides of the city. The three Metrocable lines are: Línea J from the San Javier Metro station to La Aurora in the west, Línea K from the Acevedo Metro station in the north to Santo Domingo, and Línea L from Santo Domingo to the Parque Arví. The Metrocable runs 9am-10pm daily. The Metrocable Línea L from Santo Domingo to the Parque Arví operates 9am-6pm Tuesday-Sunday. When Monday is a holiday, the Línea L runs that day and does not operate the next day, Tuesday.

Metroplús Rapid Bus

The first line of the Metroplús (www.metroplus.

gov.co) rapid bus system, with dedicated bus stops similar to those of the TransMilenio in Bogotá, debuted in 2013. There are two Metroplús lines: Línea 1 and Línea 2. Línea 1 connects the working-class neighborhood of Arjuanez in the north with the Universidad de Medellín in the southwest. Línea 2 connects the same two sectors but passes through the Centro and Plaza Mayor area. To access the system, you have to use the Tarjeta Cívica, which can be purchased at any Metro station.

Taxis

Taxis are plentiful in Medellín. Order them over the phone when possible. A few taxi companies have easy-to-remember numbers: tel. 4/444-4444, tel. 4/335-3535, and tel. 4/211-1111. Friendly Miguel Espinosa (cell tel. 311/378-3565) is a cabbie based around the Laureles area. You can also order reliable cabs using the smartphone app Tappsi.

Northern and Eastern Antioquia

SANTA FE DE ANTIOQUIA

Living and breathing colonial charm, this pueblo 80 kilometers (50 miles) northwest of Medellín is the best of Antioquia. The historic center of the town is compact, with landmarks of plazas, parks, and churches. Santa Fe was founded in 1541 by Jorge Robledo, a ruthless conquistador. An important center for gold mining, Santa Fe was capital of Antioquia until 1823, when it lost that title to Medellín. On the banks of the Río Cauca, its proximity to Medellín makes it an easy trip for those interested in seeing a colonial-era jewel of a pueblo.

With the average temperature a sizzling 27°C (81°F), it can be a challenge to fully enjoy strolling the lovely streets of the pueblo during the heat of the day. If you can, plan to go for the night (one weekday night will do), arriving in late afternoon. That's the nicest time to stroll the streets.

Sights

The town's narrow stone streets are adorned with charming plazas and parks and five historic churches. It's a delight to stroll the town in the late afternoon, after the heat of the day has subsided. Churches and historic buildings in Santa Fe are often built in the typical *calicanto* style, a mix of brick and stone construction materials. Historic colonial churches, with majestic facades, often face parks and are illuminated at night.

The "grandmother" of churches in Antioquia, the Templo de Santa Bárbara (Cl. 8 at Cra. 8, masses 7am and 6pm Mon.-Sat. 6am and 6pm Sun.), with its many baroque elements, was built towards the end of the 18th century. Next to it, in what was a Jesuit college, is the Museo de Arte Religioso (Cl. 11 No. 8-12, tel. 4/311-3808, 9am-5pm Sat.-Sun., COP$2,000), a museum that highlights paintings, sculptures, and gold and silver pieces from the Spanish New World colonies.

A nicely presented museum housed in a colonial-style house, the Museo Juan del Corral (Cl.

11 No. 9-77, tel. 4/853-4605, www.museojuandelcorral.com, 9am-noon and 2pm-5:30pm Mon.-Fri., 10am-5pm Sat.-Sun., free) has exhibits on the history of Santa Fe, including historical items from 1813 when Antioquia was declared free. The museum also puts on temporary exhibits of contemporary Colombian artists, and other cultural events are held here.

Six kilometers (four miles) outside of town, on an old road that leads to the town of Sopetrán on the other side of the Río Cauca, is an architectural wonder, the Puente de Occidente, a suspension bridge made of iron and steel. It was built towards the end of the 19th century by José María Villa, an engineer who studied in New Jersey and worked on the Brooklyn Bridge. It's a narrow bridge and has been closed to vehicular traffic, for the most part. *Mototaxis* can take you there from town, across the bridge, and back for COP$15,000. The bridge is easily reached by bike as well.

Festivals and Events

The big event in Santa Fe is the week-long Festival de Cine de Antioquia (www.festicineantioquia.com), a film festival held each year in early December. There is usually an international director or actor who is the guest of honor. Some free showings are held outdoors in the town's plazas and parks.

Accommodations

Medellín families converge on Santa Fe en masse on weekends, and for many the draw is to lounge by the pool at one of the hotels lining the main road leading into town. Hotels in town, however, have more charm. Hotel prices can drop substantially during the week.

In town, the (Hotel Mariscal Robledo (Cl. 10 No. 9-70, tel. 4/853-1111, cell tel. 313/760-0099, www.hotelmariscalrobledo.com, COP$120,000-170,000 d) is far and away the most comfortable

The historic town of Santa Fe de Antioquia makes for a pleasant overnight trip from Medellín.

hotel, and one oozing with personality. Antiques, especially with a cinematic theme, decorate the lobby and common areas. Rooms on the second floor, which have not been given a 21st-century makeover, are nonetheless comfortable, and have far more character. The pool area is luxurious.

On the boutique side, the Hotel Casa Tenerife (Cra. 8 No. 9-50, tel. 4/853-2261, www.hotelcasa-tenerife.com, COP$162,000 d) has 12 rooms, is tastefully decorated, and has a nice pool and courtyard area. It often caters to couples celebrating romantic getaways, with such details as rose petals on the bed.

On the Plaza Mayor are two options. The family-run Hotel Caserón Plaza (Cl. 9-41, Plaza Mayor, tel. 4/853-2040, www.hotelcaseronplaza.com.co, COP$145,000-208,000 d) has an excellent location but is overpriced for what you get. Some of the 33 rooms have air conditioning, which is a plus in Santa Fe. There is also a small pool in back, another plus. Hostal de la Plaza Mayor (Cra. 9 No. 9-59, tel. 4/255-7427, cell tel.

311/396-5628, http://hostalplazamayorsantaf-edeantioquia.blogspot.com, COP$50,000 d) is the budget option in town. Staff are friendly, but it's a little run down.

Food

There are few places in Colombia where one can dine to the soft tones of classical or jazz music. The Restaurante Bar La Comedia (Parque Santa Barbara, tel. 4/853-1243, noon-3pm and 6pm-10pm Wed.-Sun., COP$18,000) is one such place. Light dishes, sandwiches, and crêpes dominate the small menu, and this is also an option for late afternoon *onces,* tea time. It's diagonal to the Santa Bárbara church. Restaurante Portón del Parque (Cl. 10 No. 11-03, tel. 4/853-3207, noon-8pm Sun.-Thurs., noon-9:30pm Sat.-Sun., COP$20,000) is lavishly decorated with portraits and paintings by owner Olga Cecilia. In addition to typical Paisa specialties (lunch specials during the week go for under COP$10,000), the extensive menu offers seafood and international cuisine. Finally, the restaurant at the Hotel Mariscal Robledo (Cl. 10 No. 9-70, tel. 4/853-1111, cell tel. 313/760-0099, www.hotelmar-iscalrobledo.com, 8am-3pm and 7pm-10pm daily, COP$25,000) is always a good choice.

Recreation

Naturaventura (Hotel Mariscal Robledo, Cl. 10 No. 9-70, tel. 4/853-1946, naturaventura1@hotmail.com) organizes nature walks, bike trips, horseback riding, and rafting excursions. For horseback riding, contact Guías Turantioquia (tel. 4/853-1148), which organizes day-trip horseback riding tours in and around Santa Fe.

Shopping

Spaniards were once attracted to Santa Fe because of its gold. Today it is famous for its intricate filigree jewelry. To peruse some, visit ORFOA (Cl. 9 No. 6-02, tel. 4/853-2880, 9am-noon and 2pm-6pm daily) or Dulces & Artesanías Clavellina (Hotel Mariscal Robledo, Cl. 10 No. 9-70, tel. 4/853-2195, 9am-noon and 2pm-6pm daily). Clavellina is the symbolic flower of Santa Fe.

Guarnielería y Marroquinería (Cl. 10 No. 7-66, cell tel. 314/847-8354, noon-7pm Mon.-Fri., 10am-7pm Sat.-Sun.) sells authentic Jericó *carrieles* (shoulder bags used by Paisa cowhands) and other locally made leather handicrafts. **La Casa Solariega** (Cl. de la Amargura No. 8-09, tel. 4/853-1530, 9am-noon and 2pm-6pm daily) has an eclectic collection of handicrafts, paintings, and antiques in a typical Santa Fe house.

Information and Services
A tourist information office on the Plaza Mayor (Cra. 9 and Cl. 9, tel. 4/853-1022) has maps and hotel information.

Getting There and Around
There is regular bus service, several times a day, from the Terminal de Transportes del Norte (Cra. 64 No. 78-344, tel. 4/267-7075, www.terminalesmmedellin.com) in Medellín to Santa Fe. The journey takes two hours and takes you through a feat of modern engineering: the Túnel Fernando Gómez Martínez, the longest tunnel in South America. To return, walk a couple of blocks to the Medellín-Turbo highway near the market at Carrera 10 and flag down passing buses. Most of them are going to Medellín. The trip costs under COP$10,000.

MAGDALENA MEDIO
◖ Reserva Natural Río Claro
A visit to the spectacular, privately run Reserva Natural Río Claro (Medellín office tel. 4/268-8855, cell tel. 311/354-0119, www.rioclaroelrefugio.com) is a highlight for anyone visiting Colombia. In the steamy and remote Magdalena Medio region of Antioquia, the reserve encompasses 450 hectares (1,100 acres) along the Río Claro canyon, a babbling, crystal-clear river. This reserve is a place to enjoy the unspoiled beauty of the river and its jungle and to disconnect from the hectic pace of urban life.

The story behind the park begins with an oft-repeated tale about a pesky jaguar. It seems that the cat was blamed for killing some livestock of a campesino in the area. In a quest to track down the guilty party (the jaguar got away unharmed), the farmer followed its tracks through the jungle, over several days, and to a spectacular canyon. When Juan Guillermo Garcés heard about the astonishing discovery, he had to see this undiscovered territory for himself. Garcés immediately knew that this was a special place, and he made a commitment to purchase the land to protect it from development, including a highway that was to pass through this pristine land.

On weekends, Río Claro receives many visitors. In addition to those staying at the reserve, many day visitors spend the afternoon at Río Claro. Don't go on a Saturday, Sunday, or holiday if you seek a peaceful commune with nature. If you visit the reserve midweek, you'll most likely have the place practically to yourself, which is heavenly.

RECREATION
Guides don't speak English, generally. There are two must-do activities at the reserve. The first is an easy rafting trip down the river (COP$20,000), during which you can see the karstic jungle, in which trees grow atop rocks. This excursion takes about two hours. The second must-do activity is a combination swim/hike trip to the Caverna de los Guácharos (COP$15,000 pp). This guided walk has its challenging moments: wading across the swiftly flowing river, making your way through the dark, dark cavern, climbing out of the cavern, and then making your way back across the river. *Guácharo* birds (oilbirds), living inside the cavern, act like they own the place (the cavern is, after all, named for them). They don't like it when human intruders invade their space, and they'll let you know that with their screeching. The cavern is made of marble; its stalactites and stalagmites are impressive. Waterproof shoes with good traction are recommended, as you'll be wading in water most of the time. Also, it's nice to have a headlamp so that you'll have hands free. You can take your camera, but at a certain point it will need to be kept in a water repellent bag, which the guide will have. If you're up for both trips, go on

© ANDREW DIER

Reserva Natural Río Claro

the cavern tour in the morning and go rafting in the late afternoon.

Other activities at the reserve include rock-climbing, a zip line, hanging out on the marble beach, self-guided nature walks, and tubing. These are all arranged by Río Claro staff.

ACCOMMODATIONS

The reserve has a variety of accommodations options. Contact the Río Claro office (tel. 4/268-8855, cell tel. 311/354-0119, www.rioclaroelrefugio.com) for all reservations and information. The Hotel El Refugio (COP$80,000) is above the reception and dining area, and is a comfortable all-wooden lodge construction. The best and most isolated is at the far end near the canyon, a 15-minute walk from the main reception area in the Cabañas El Refugio (COP$95,000-140,000 pp), where rooms are quite spectacular and open-air. You'll sleep well here with the sounds of the rushing water to lull you asleep. Rooms are completely open, but there are no problems with mosquitoes.

The Hotel Río Claro (COP$95,000 pp) is across the highway from the rest of the reserve but still along the river, and it has a big pool. These are small concrete bungalows. The hotel is popular with student groups. All meals are included in the room rates. Tell staff when you make your reservation if you have any dietary needs or special requests, like fresh fruit.

GETTING THERE

The reserve is easily reached by bus from Medellín. All buses between Medellín and Bogotá pass in front of the Río Claro entrance, where there is a small security booth. From Medellín, it takes around three hours, costing around COP$20,000. Be sure to tell the driver you'd like to be dropped off at the *"entrada de la Reserva Río Claro."* ("the entrance to the Río Claro Reserve").

Hacienda Napoles

The Hacienda Napoles (Puerto Triunfo, cell tel. 314/892-2307, www.haciendanapoles.com, 9am-6pm Tues.-Sun., COP$32,000) was a vacation home for Pablo Escobar, complete with an airstrip and exotic animals, including quite a few hippos, who apparently adapted nicely to the muggy climes of the Río Magdalena area. Today Hacienda Napoles is a theme park with giant dinosaur sculptures, some of which were built by Escobar for his children; two water parks (additional fees); hippopotami, zebras, and ostriches; an Africa museum; the remnants of Pablo Escobar's country house (now a museum); a collection of old cars that were destroyed following his death; and his private airplane landing strip.

Avoid the oppressive heat and intense sun of midday (and the crowds on weekends) by visiting early on a weekday morning. The park can easily be visited from Río Claro, which is about an hour away. When Monday is a holiday, the park closes on Tuesday rather than on Monday.

GUATAPE

The stone monolith La Piedra dominates the landscape here, but the Guatape area is more than just a big rock: It's a weekend playground chock full of recreational activities that keep the crowds from Medellín busy.

Sights

Guatape is a resort town. Aside from La Piedra, it's known for its *zócalos,* colorful designs of the friezes on the lower part of houses. Many of these honor the traditions of townspeople, such as farming and fishing, others have sheep or other animals, and still others hot rods or Pink Panther. A particularly colorful street is the Calle del Recuerdos near the Parque Principal.

On a serene mountainside near Guatape, beyond El Encuentro hostel on the same road is the Monasterio Santa María de la Epifanía (www. monjesbenedictinosguatape.org), home to around 30 Benedictine monks. Guests, up to eight at a time, are welcome to stay. Every day of the week at the 5:15pm *vísperas* (vespers) service, the public is invited to hear the monks sing Gregorian chants.

Check out the Iglesia de Piedra in the town of El Peñol, a modern construction that resembles La Piedra, which is quite a strange sight.

La Piedra Peñol

Known simply as La Piedra, La Piedra Peñol (8am-6pm daily, COP$10,000) is a giant rock monolith that soars 200 meters (650 feet) into the sky from the scenic and meandering Embalse Peñol-Guatape, an important reservoir covering some 64 square kilometers (25 square miles) that is an important producer of hydro-electric energy for the country. There's been quite a rivalry between the towns of El Peñol and Guatape over the years, over which town can claim La Piedra for their own. It is located between the two, a tad closer to the Guatape side. Things digressed to a point where folks from Guatape began to paint their town's name in large letters on one prominent side of the rock. People from El Peñol were not amused, and this giant marking of territory was halted by authorities. Today all that remains of that brouhaha is what appear to be the letters "GI."

The 360-degree views from the top of La Piedra over the Guatape reservoir and Antioqiuan countryside are worth the toil of climbing up over 600 steps, in a ramshackle brick and concrete stairwell that is stuck to the rock, to the top. To celebrate your feat, you can have a drink at one of the snack bars there.

In front of La Piedra, there is a statue of the man who first climbed the monolith in 1954. Inspired by a priest, Luis Villegas López and two friends took five days to slowly climb up cracks in the rock. They had to deal with a beehive and a rainstorm along the way, adding to the challenge. It's one of the top tourist attractions in Antioquia. From the bottom of the rock, look up and notice the hundreds of bromeliads growing along the sides of it.

La Piedra can be visited several ways. You can walk from Guatape, which takes 45 minutes. (Sunscreen and water are essential.) You can bike it, although the road that winds its way up to the rock entrance is quite steep. You can take a *mototaxi* from your hotel (COP$10,000), or you can hop on a Jeep from the Parque Principal (between Cras. 28-29 and Clls. 31-32) in Guatape. It's best to make your visit during the early morning hours or late in the afternoon due to potent sun rays.

The town is surrounded by a large reservoir operated by EPM, the Medellín utility company. The reservoir was built in phases during the 1970s and was not without controversy, as the flooding of the area began without the full consent of the inhabitants. Finally all families were resettled by EPM by 1979, and the town of El Peñol gradually became covered with rising waters, with only a church steeple remaining as a reminder of the town's past.

Tours

A popular excursion is to take a boat tour with brothers Luis and Rodolfo Londoño (cell tel. 312/794-7150 or 312/236-5783, COP$50,000-100,000 per boat) to some of the islands of the reservoir. A standard stop on the tour is to (or rather, above) the submerged town of Viejo Peñol. It was flooded on purpose during the construction of the reservoir and nearby dam in 1978. The only real remnant of the town is a large cross rising out of the water. A small historical museum displays old photos and historical memorabilia from the old town on the waterside. These tours typically last 45 minutes to 1.5 hours.

Accommodations

During the week, prices drop significantly at most hotels, especially if you pay in cash.

El Encuentro (tel. 4/861-1374, cell tel. 311/619-6199, www.hostalelencuentro.com, COP$20,000 dorm, COP$65,000 d), a 12-minute walk up from town, remains one of the best options in Guatape. Run by a friendly Californian named Greg, the hostel is on the Guatape-Peñol reservoir, and rooms are spread throughout two houses, with about 10 rooms in total. Most of these are private rooms, and some have a shared bath. A larger apartment and two dorms are available here, as well as a place for tents down by the lake. The staff at El Encuentro can organize a plethora of outdoorsy things to do: downhill mountain bike rides on their excellent bikes, hikes, and jumping off of bridges. Spanish classes can be arranged, and you can study your verbs on the nice deck.

In town is the newer Tomate Café Hostel (Cl. 30 No. 28-120, tel. 4/861-1100, cell tel. 312/216-1199, www.tomatecafehostel.com, COP$18,000 dorm, COP$40,000 d). It's run by a Paisa family and has four small private rooms and two dorm rooms. A strong cup of coffee is always on offer here, as well as healthy and vegetarian food in their restaurant. It's next to a disco, so on weekend nights it can get thumping. You were warned!

At Mi Casa Guatape (tel. 4/861-0632, cell tel. 301/457-5726, www.micasaguatape.com, COP$20,000 dorm, COP$60,000 d) guests wake up, step outside with a cup of coffee in hand, and greet their neighbor, La Piedra, with a warm *Buenos días*. You can't get much closer to that big rock than from this small English-Colombian hostel. The hostel has five private rooms and one four-bed dorm as well as two kitchens for use. When not outdoors climbing La Piedra or taking out their kayak for a spin, guests can laze in hammocks on the deck, watch movies, or bond with the owners' sweet dog. Mi Casa works closely with Adventure Activities (cell tel. 301/411-4442), just next door, a group that organizes an intense-rock climbing excursion up one of dozens of routes up La Piedra (COP$60,000, 7 hours), as well as other outings. Owner Sean takes guests on a waterfall hike (6 km/4 miles round-trip, COP$15,000, 4 hours). It's easy to go into town from the hostel by catching a ride with a passing Jeep or with Mi Casa's preferred *mototaxi* driver. Mi Casa is about three kilometers before Guatape on the main road (25-min. walk or COP$1,500 taxi ride) and is across the street from landmark El Estadero La Mona.

There are a couple of upscale hotels in town. Hotel Portobello (Cl. 32 No. 28-29, tel. 4/861-0016, cell tel. 312/783-4050, www.hotelportobeloguatape.com, COP$215,000 d) has 16 rooms, and most of them have a view of the lake. You can obtain a 25 percent discount during the week if you pay in cash.

Food

Fish like massive carp and trout from the reservoir are the specialty in Guatape. Reliable fish and

Colombian cuisine restaurants include La Fogata (Cra. 30 No. 31-32, tel. 4/861-1040, cell tel. 314/740-7282, 8am-8pm daily), on the waterfront.

Pizza and pasta are on the menu at Rafaelos (below Hotel Portobello on the waterfront, tel. 4/861-0016, cell tel. 310/200-9020, 11am-11pm Wed.-Sun.).

Craving a curry? ◖ Donde Sam (El Peñol, near church, tel. 4/851-5401, cell tel. 320/667-5870, 11am-11pm daily, COP$15,000) is worth the trip. Owner and chef Sam, from Agra, and his Colombian wife, Lina, serve up authentic Indian dishes (as well as other international cuisine). Lunches, like curry vegetables or chicken, are accompanied by a soup and salad. It's livelier at night, and sometimes they put on mood-setting music in an attempt to transport the crowd to Asia.

Sometimes exceptional hospitality can give one a sugar headache. That's what happens at Gloria Elena's generous candy tastings at Dulces de Guatape (Cl. 29 No. 23C-32, Barrio Villa del Carmen, tel. 4/861-0724, 7am-6pm). At this small candy factory, they make all kinds of sweets, many with *arequipe* (caramel) and some with fruits like the tart *uchuva* and guava as well as some chocolate bonbons that have peanuts and almonds.

Getting There and Around

There is frequent bus service from Medellín's north terminal to Guatape. The trip takes about two hours and costs COP$12,000. Buses depart Guatape at a bus terminal that was completed in 2013 on the waterfront. It's just one block from the main plaza. Buses returning to Medellín often fill up in a hurry on Sundays, especially during holidays. If you are relying on public transportation, book your return bus trip early. The last bus for Medellín departs at 6pm. The return fare is also COP$12,000.

Southern Antioquia

◖ JARDÍN

Sometimes place names fit perfectly. Such is the case in the picture-perfect Antioquian town of Jardín. The main park gushes year-round with trees and flowers always in bloom, and the streets are corridors of color as well, with brightly painted houses one after another.

For many years this town has been a favorite country getaway for Paisas from Medellín. It's becoming popular with international travelers, too, but still, if you arrive during the week, you'll feel like you've stumbled upon something special. On weekends, and especially on holidays, a festive atmosphere fills the air, and the Plaza Principal buzzes with activity.

While the main selling points of Jardín are its good looks, nearby tropical forests and cloud forests, home to natural attractions such as the Caverna El Esplendor and the ProAves bird-watching reserve, provide good excuses for lacing up those hiking boots.

Sights

The Parque Principal is the center of life in Jardín. It's full of colorful wooden chairs, eight flower gardens, a handful of tall trees that provide welcome shade, and a constant cast of characters passing through, hanging out, or sipping a coffee. Prominent on the east side of the park is the neo-gothic cathedral the Basílica Menor de la Inmaculada Concepción (Cra. 3 No. 10-71, mass daily 11am), a 20th-century construction, the striking interior of which is painted shades of turquoise.

The Museo Clara Rojas (Cra. 5 No. 9-31, tel. 6/845-5652, http://mcrpjardin.blogspot.com, 8am-noon and 2pm-6pm, COP$2,000) has 19th-century period furniture and relics from the *colonización antioqueña,* as well as a small collection of religious art, including a painting of Jesus as a child

the Parque Principal in pretty Jardín

surrounded by lambs with medals hanging around their necks. The town's tourism office is behind the museum, operating the same hours as the museum.

Recreation

Walking around Jardín is a pleasant way to get to know the town and surrounding mountains. Setting out for a walk towards the surrounding western mountains, to the Alto de las Flores or Salto del Ángel, makes for a great morning. If you lose your way, ask for directions. On the east side of town, there is a charming path, the Camino Herrera, which leads to the Casa de los Fundadores. In that area are several coffee plantations.

Jardín has not one, but two mini chairlifts in town. The Cable Aereo (8am-6pm daily, COP$5,000 round-trip) goes up to the Cristo Rey hill. The other, more rustic La Garrucha (8am-6pm daily, COP$4,000), goes across town. Although these are popular with tourists, they were built with a purpose in mind: so that rural farmers

would have an easier way to bring their coffee and other crops to market.

Condor de los Andes (tel. 4/845-5374, cell tel. 311/746-1985, condordelosandes@colombia.com) is a tourism operator that organizes walks, paragliding, and waterfall rappelling. Their most popular activity is a day-long rappelling adventure to the Caverna El Esplendor. This cavern in the jungle outside of town is reached on foot (about a 1.5-hour walk). Once there you rappel down a 50-meter-high (164-foot-high) waterfall into the cavern. Transportation and lunch are included in the price (COP$95,000 pp), and they usually depart Jardín at around 8am, returning by 4pm. The group also offers paragliding (COP$75,000, 25 mins.) and rappelling at the 53-meter-high (174-foot-high) Cascada Escalera (COP$55,000). Condor de los Andes has a small hostel (COP$35,000 pp) five blocks from the Parque Principal.

Those with an inner cowboy may want to take a horseback tour to the Salto del Ángel waterfall.

Contact John Jairo (cell tel. 312/825-4524) to reserve your spot.

The mountains that envelop most of Jardín are protected lands encompassing some 28,000 hectares (69,000 acres). This area is called the Reserva Cuchilla Jardín Tamesis. Within the reserve are caverns, waterfalls, caves, and nature paths. The park office (Alcaldía building, 2nd floor, Cra. 3 No. 10-10, tel. 4/845-5668, cell tel. 321/758-7534, dmicuchilla@corantioquia.gov.co) offers free guided walks to these natural attractions.

BIRDING

Colombia's premier bird-watching and conservation group, ProAves (www.proaves.org), operates a bird-watching park, the Reserva Natural de las Loro Orejiamarillo, within Reserva Cuchilla Jardín Tamesis. This is where the yellow ear parrot *(Ognorhynchus icterotis)* can be seen, an endangered species in Colombia. They make their nests in the majestic *palma de cera* (wax palm) trees. Another exotic bird to look for is the *colibrí de frontino (Coeligena orina)*, a species of hummingbird. In addition to birdlife, there have been spottings of pumas, the *oso de anteojos* (an Andean bear), and deer.

It is ideal to get an early start to view the parrots—as early as 5am. As the elevation is fairly high, the temperatures dip as low as 4°C (39°F). Rubber boots and warm clothing are essential.

To coordinate a visit to the bird-watching park, contact EcoTurs (Cra. 20 No. 36-61, Bogotá, tel. 1/287-6592, www.ecoturs.org) in advance as staff are not always at the site. This tour agency manages visits to this and all of the other ProAves reserves across the country. In Jardín, contact Joana Villa (cell tel. 312/867-1740), or contact Angela Gómez in Bogotá (cell tel. 313/852-9158) for more information about this park in Antioquia. There is a COP$15,000 entrance fee per person for Reserva Natural de las Loro Orejiamarillo; a guide service costs COP$50,000 per group; and round-trip jeep transportation along rugged mountain roads to the reserve is a whopping COP$240,000.

Devils of Riosucio

Every two years in January, in the sleepy coffee- and plantain-growing town Riosucio in northern Caldas near the Antioquian town of Jardín, residents (and a growing number of visitors) go to the devil during the revelry of the Carnaval de Riosucio. This festival, one of the most beloved in the region, has an interesting story. It began out of a plea made by local priests for two feuding pueblos of Riosucio—the gold-mining village of Quiebralomo and La Montaña, home to a large indigenous population—to get along. In 1847 both communities were nudged to participate in that year's Three Kings Day commemoration and to set aside their differences, temporarily at least. If they didn't come together that year in peace, they would invite the wrath of the devil.

Over time, it was that last bit that resonated with the townspeople. From that year onward, groups of families, friends, and neighbors would get together and create elaborate floats and costumes, seemingly in homage to the devil over this five-day celebration. The festival is run by the República del Carnaval, which reigns over the town during that time, and the culmination of the event is the ceremonial burning of an effigy of the devil. The festival gets going on the first Friday of January with the most colorful activities taking place on Sunday.

La Esperanza (cell tel. 312/837-0782, COP$180,000 pp all meals incl.) is a private nature reserve run by an American, Doug Knapp, set on a mountain ridge 15 minutes from town. Sunrises, with a view to Jardín, and sunsets, looking out towards the mountains of Los Farallones del Citaró, can't be beat. A Jack of many trades, birder Knapp built three comfortable cabins complete with siesta-friendly decks and natural light pouring through the windows. He's also carved out some forest paths that meander through the property. Oh, and he cooks, too.

At La Esperanza, you don't have to go far to catch a glimpse of some spectacular birds. Knapp's colleagues have documented the presence of eight endemic birds, including the Parker's antbird, the whiskered wren, the Colombian chacalaca, and the yellow-headed manakin. More than 365 species are estimated to live in the Jardín area.

Accommodations

If you are planning to visit Jardín on a *puente* (long weekend) or during holidays, you will need to make a reservation at a hotel well in advance. On regular weekends, there is usually no problem in finding a hotel, although the best options do tend to fill up. During the week, the town is yours, and prices drop substantially (especially if you plan to pay in cash).

Although Jardín has plenty of reasonably priced hotel options, there is just one hostel. ❰ Casa Selva y Café (Casa del Lago Vereda La Salada, tel. 4/845-5430, cell tel. 318/518-7171, www.hostal-selvaycafe.com, COP$25,000 dorm, COP$50,000-90,000 d) is a cozy countryside spot, about a 12-minute walk away from the hustle and bustle of Jardín city life. Back behind a little pond surrounded with flowers and fruit trees with pastureland and mountains behind, it is pure peace here. Alexandra, the owner, is a yoga teacher and gives classes on-site every Tuesday and Thursday, which are free for hostel guests. For nonguests the classes cost COP$20,000. The two private rooms and two dorms are spacious and clean with high ceilings and hardwood floors.

Hotel Casa Grande (Cl. 8 No. 4-33, tel. 4/845-5487, cell tel. 311/340-2207, www.hotelcasagrande.co, COP$30,000 pp) features 12 rooms, which have a capacity of 2-5 persons each. Most rooms have 2-4 beds to accommodate families. Breakfast is included in the price, and dinner can be arranged at the hotel as well. The friendly owner, a Jardín native, can supply tourist information for the area.

Hotel Valdivia Plaza (Parque Principal, next to the Museo Clara Rojas, tel. 4/845-5055, cell tel. 316/528-1047, COP$58,000 d) has 20 rooms and is clean, but isn't bursting with personality. Splurge for a room with a private balcony overlooking the park.

Hotel Jardín (Cra. 3 No. 9-14, cell tel. 310/380-6724, COP$40,000 pp) has 11 spacious and modern

apartments with a capacity of 4-8 persons each. It's a bargain. This is the most colorful house in a most colorful town, with orange, yellow, red, and blue balconies, doors, and trim. The house was restored in 2012.

A comfortable, if conservative, choice is Comfenalco Hotel Hacienda Balandú (Km. 1 Vía Jardín Riosucio, tel. 4/845-5561, COP$158,000 d), a hotel with all the extras: restaurant, sauna, and swimming pool. It's a tranquil 15- to 20-minute walk from town.

Food

The soft glow of candlelight at ❰ Café Europa (Cl. 8 No. 4-02, cell tel. 312/230-2842, 11am-3pm and 6pm-10pm Wed.-Mon.) is hard to resist for weekenders. This corner restaurant run by a German photographer and travel writer serves nice pizzas. Order a bottle of French wine (COP$35,000) and settle in. There's no rush in Jardín. The menu at Pastelatte (Cra. 4 No. 8-45, cell tel. 301/482-3908, noon-8:30pm Wed.-Mon., COP$14,000) features crêpes, cheesecakes, coffee, sandwiches, and pastas, and service is speedy and always with a smile. Zodiaco (off the main plaza in front of the Hotel El Dorado, tel. 4/845-5615, 8am-11pm daily, COP$15,000) is a *comida típica* (Colombian fare) restaurant, but it's a couple of notches fancier than most restaurants in town.

At Las Margaritas (Cra. 3 No. 9-68, tel. 4/845-6651, 7am-9pm daily, COP$15,000), the specialty is *pollo a la Margarita* (chicken fried with a Parmesan cheese breading). This back-to-Paisa-basics place is good for a hearty breakfast. Vegetarians will appreciate a generous morning serving of *calentado* (beans and rice). If you want to add some juice (not a part of the typical Paisa breakfast), there is a juice stall two doors down from Las Margaritas, as well as fruit vendors in the park. The *tienda* (store) next door often has fresh Colombian pastries, such as *almojabanas* (cheese rolls) and *pandebonos* (delicious pastries made of yuca flour and cheese).

It's a weekend ritual in Jardín: spend the afternoon with family and friends at one of the *trucheras* (trout farms). One of the largest and best known of these is La Truchería (Km. 5 Vía Riosucio, tel. 4/845-5159, noon-6pm daily, COP$18,000). Trout is served infinite ways here: *a la mostaza* (mustard), with fine herbs, and stuffed with vegetables, to name a few. And what better way to round out the day than with a rousing paintball game!

The Café de los Andes (Parque Principal, Cra. 5 No. 9-73, tel. 4/845-6239, 8:30am-9pm Thurs.-Mon., 9:30am-8pm Tues.-Wed.) is the brew of choice from Jardín, and their café on the terrace of the Casa del Café is the finest spot in Jardín for a caffeine jolt. Go for an espresso; other coffee drinks are disappointingly weak. It's in the Casa del Café; if you go upstairs you might see the bean-to-bag process in action.

Dulces del Jardín (Cl. 13 No. 5-47, tel. 4/845-6584, www.dulcesdejardin.com, 8am-6pm Mon.-Sat.) is the candy-maker in town. In addition to *arequipe* (caramel) sweets, they make all-natural jams and fruit spreads (COP$6,000) from pineapple, coconut, and papaya.

Siglo XXI (Cra. 6 No. 9-18, no phone, noon-8pm daily) is a hole in the wall where you can have a beer and brush shoulders with locals. The walls of this pub are decorated with faded photos of the town and of local *futbolistas* (soccer players).

Getting There and Around

The bus company Transportes Suroeste Antioqueño (tel. 4/352-9049, COP$18,000) leaves Medellín each day bound for Jardín, leaving from the Terminal de Transportes Sur.

There is also one bus at 6:30am that leaves for Manizales to the south in the coffee region from Jardín. This route goes through the town of Riosucio.

JERICÓ

Jericó and Jardín are two (colorfully painted) peas in the same pod. Both are fiercely traditional Paisa pueblos, and they won't change for anybody. Although it is the closer of the two to Medellín, Jericó feels more remote, and

less visited, and therein lies its charm. Set on a gentle slope of a mountain overlooking a valley dotted with cattle ranches and farms of coffee, tomato, plantain, and, cardamom, Jericó still is very much a Paisa cowboy outpost. Colombians know Jericó for two very different reasons. The first is its unique handicraft, the *carriel,* a shoulder bag made out of leather and cowhide that is a symbol of Paisa cowboy culture. The second is its homegrown saint, Laura Montoya, who was canonized in 2013.

Jericó is a pleasant place to hang one's (cowboy) hat for a night, and its sleepy streets lined with brightly colored wooden balconies and doors are a playground for shutterbugs.

Sights

The Catedral de Nuestra Señora de las Mercedes (Cl. 7 No. 4-34, Plaza de Bolívar, tel. 4/852-3494) is a brick construction that towers over the Parque Reyes. The cathedral is where Laura Montoya was officially declared a saint (Colombia's first) during a ceremony in May 2013. Born into poverty in 1874, Montoya was raised by her grandmother. She began her adulthood as a teacher but later decided to enter religious service. Montoya set out on a lengthy missionary mission into the jungle to witness to indigenous people. She later started a religious order that focused on marginalized peoples that has since spread to many countries. Two miracles are attributed to Montoya. At the entrance to the cathedral, there is a bronze statue of the saint alongside an indigenous child, representing Montoya's devotion to assisting impoverished communities in remote areas.

Below the cathedral is the Museo de Arte Religioso (Cl. 7 No. 4-34, Plaza de Bolívar, tel. 4/852-3494, 8:30am-noon and 1:30pm-6pm Mon.-Fri., 8:30am-6pm Sat., 9am-noon and 1:30pm-5:30pm Sun., COP$2,000), in which religious art and ceremonial items from the colonial period onwards are on display. Often the museum hosts temporary art exhibitions.

The best museum in town, and probably

© ANDREW DIER

the colorful Paisa town of Jericó

the best outside of Medellín, is the Museo de Jericó Antioquia (Cl. 7 between Cras. 5-6, tel. 4/852-4045, cell tel. 311/628-8325, 8am-noon and 1:30pm-6pm Mon.-Fri., 9am-5pm Sat.-Sun., COP$2,000). This museum has several rooms, with some dedicated to archaeology (ceramics and other items from the Emberá indigenous group of western Colombia) and the rest to contemporary art from Antioquian artists. The museum also shows films during the week, and concerts featuring a range of musical genres are held on the last weekend of each month.

On the Morro El Salvador, or Cerro de Cristo Rey (called this because of the white statue of Christ on a pedestal), four blocks from the plaza, is the Jardín Botánico Los Balsos, a small botanical garden. For COP$8,000 round-trip you can take a *teleférico* (gondola) to the Parque Las Nubes, a park on a hill overlooking Jericó. The park is also known as the Parque Los Venados (Deer Park) for its many four-legged residents. Some short paths lead to a waterfall and to a grotto, and the views of the town and Antioquian countryside

are sweeping. Neither the garden nor the park has an entry fee, and they are open to the public daily from sunrise to sunset.

Shopping

To find your very own *carriel* shoulder bag or other leather souvenir from Jericó, walk down Carrera 5. On the righthand side of the street are a couple of classic shops like Guarnielería Jericó (Cra. 5 No. 5-35, tel. 4/852-3370, 9am-6pm daily) and Taller de Guarnielería & Talabartería (Cra. 5 No. 5-03, tel. 4/852-3128, cell tel. 311/716-9895, 9am-6pm daily). The classic *carriel* goes for about COP$130,000. Oddly, you probably won't see many people other than tourists actually using these unique handbags. *Carrieles* were used by *arrieros* (Paisa cowboys) for their horseback trips around Tierra Paisa. These bags are accordion-like, with several divisions in them for carrying items like money, a lock of hair, a knife, or a candle. Some suspect that the name *carriel* is derived from the English "carry all," while others say it comes from the French *cartier,* or handbag.

On the same street is a sweets store, Delicias del Cardamomo (Cra. 5 No. 2-128, tel. 4/852-5289, 9am-6pm daily) that sells cardamom candies, cardamom cookies, and plain old cardamom seeds. Cardamom is a relatively important crop in Jericó.

Accommodations

As in all Colombian pueblos, room rates drop during the week.

The best value in town is the Casa Grande (Cl. 7 No. 5-54, tel. 4/852-3229, cell tel. 311/329-2144, www.hotelcasagrande.freshcreator.com, COP$40,000 pp). It's a nicely renovated old house with 15 simple rooms. Rooms facing the street are preferable. Hotel Portón Plaza (Cl. 7 No. 3-25, tel. 4/852-3009, www.hotelportonplaza.com, COP$35,000 pp) runs a close second, although it's much larger. It is just off of the plaza. Ask for room 209 for a good view, or a second-floor room with a view over the street.

Food

On the Parque Principal there are quite a few restaurant and café options along its east side. On late afternoons, the entire length of one side of the plaza is full of folks enjoying a *tinto* (coffee) and watching the comings and goings of townspeople milling about the plaza. A meal with a view is the selling point of El Balcón Restaurante (Parque Principal, Cra. 4 No. 6-26, tel. 4/852-3191, cell tel. 311/784-4419, 8am-9pm daily, COP$15,000). From its perch on a balcony, you have front row seats to the action below in the plaza and a nice vista of the mountains in the distance. The Colombian dishes are filling.

Mandala (Cl. 7 No. 5-55, tel. 4/852-3331, 7am-10pm daily, COP$15,000) is as funky as it gets in Jerico. This restaurant, which serves everything from paella to Colombian comfort food, is also a hangout spot where live music is sometimes on offer. Casa Gourmet (Cl. 7 No. 3-16, tel. 4/852-4323, 11am-10pm daily, COP$15,000), across from the Hotel Portón Plaza, serves fast food like pizza, burgers, and crêpes. "Gourmet" is a bit of a stretch, but if you're looking for a quick meal that strays from the rigid *comida típica* fare, this will do.

Information and Services

There is a small tourist booth (tel. 4/852-852-3101, cell tel. 321/612-3743, www.jericoturistico.com, 9am-6pm Thurs.-Tues.) across from the Catedral de Nuestra Señora de las Mercedes. You can get information on hotels, restaurants, and things to do. They also sell sweets, like *crema de solteras,* a typical sweet from Jericó, and cardamom candies, as well as handicrafts. The tourist office organizes walking tours of the town in Spanish on weekends. Inquire at the office or contact guide Maribel (cell tel. 313/672-0199).

Getting There and Around

There is regular bus service to Jericó from the Terminal del Sur in Medellín (COP$20,000), starting at 5am and going until 6pm. Buses arrive and depart from the Parque Principal. To get to Jardín from Jericó, you must take a *chiva* (rural bus) to the town of Andes or to the town of Peñalisa and transfer there to Jardín.

The Coffee Region

Blessed by lush, tropical vegetation, meticulously manicured countryside dotted with beautiful haciendas and towns, spring-like weather, and a backdrop of massive, snowcapped mountains, Colombia's coffee region is almost Eden. Nature here is a thousand shades of green: bright green bamboo groves, emerald colored forests with spots of white *yarumo* trees, dark green coffee groves, and green-blue mountains in the distance punctuated by brightly colored flowers and polychromatic butterflies and birds.

Though the main cities and many towns lack charm, dozens of well-preserved villages offer colorful balcony-clad buildings. Life in most of these towns remains untouched by tourism. A visit on market day, with bustling streets jammed with Jeeps, burdened people, and goods, is a memorable one.

And then there is coffee. It is true that Brazil and Vietnam are the world's top coffee producers, but arabica beans are grown throughout Colombia. Coffee grown in some parts of the country (such as Cauca and Nariño) is considered superior to that from this region, but here, more than anywhere else, coffee is an inseparable part of Paisa identity. While the extent of land devoted to coffee farming is diminishing, the numbers are still impressive: The department of Caldas contains over 80,000 hectares (200,000 acres) of coffee farms; Risaralda, 52,000 hectares (128,000 acres); and Quindío, 30,000 hectares (74,000 acres). Visit a coffee farm to understand the laborious production process or—even better—stay overnight.

History

In pre-Columbian times, this region was inhabited by the Quimbaya people. In 1537, Spanish conquistador Sebastián de Belalcázar conquered the region as he moved north from Ecuador towards the central Muisca region. Due to the sparse indigenous population and lack of precious metals, the region, which was governed from faraway Popayán, was largely uninhabited during most of the colonial period.

The Birth of the Coffee Economy

During the 19th century, demographic pressures spurred settlers from the northwestern province of Antioquia to migrate south, giving origin to what is known as the *colonización antioqueña*. For this reason, the coffee region is akin to Antioquia, with similar dialect, cuisine, and architecture. As the settlers made their way south, they founded towns and started farms: Salamina was established in 1825, Manizales in 1849, Filandia in 1878, and Armenia in 1889.

The region prospered enormously throughout the 20th century due to ideal conditions for producing coffee. The Colombian National Coffee Federation, owner of the Juan Valdez brand, provided technical assistance, developed infrastructure, and helped stabilize prices. High international coffee prices during the 1980s and 1990s made the region one of the most prosperous areas in the country.

The fall of global coffee prices in the past decade has forced the region to reinvent itself. Rather than produce a low-value commodity, many farmers have invested in producing high-quality strains that fetch much higher prices. Growers have also diversified, planting other crops, such as plantains, often interspersed through coffee plantations. Finally, agro- and eco-tourism has provided a much-needed new source of revenue.

Planning Your Time

It's hard to go wrong as a tourist in the coffee region. No matter your starting point or home base, an immersion in coffee culture is easy, nearby, and rewarding. If you can, plan to spend about five days in this most pleasant part of Colombia. In that time you can stay at a coffee hacienda, visit a natural park, and tour a picture-perfect pueblo.

However, if time is short, a quick visit can be equally as rewarding. With easy transportation links to the major cities of the region and excellent tourism infrastructure to meet all budget needs, Salento has the trifecta of coffee region attractions: It's a cute pueblo, coffee farms are within minutes of the main plaza, and jungle hikes that lead through tropical forest to the Valle de Cocora are easy to organize. The town gets packed with visitors on weekends and during holidays, resulting in a more festive atmosphere, but also traffic jams.

Another option is to stay a couple of days at a hacienda. You can leisurely explore the farms and countryside, relax, and possibly go for a day trip or two to a nearby attraction. Many haciendas are high-end, like Hacienda Bambusa, Finca Villa Nora, and Hacienda San José. However, budget travelers can also enjoy the unique atmosphere of hacienda life at Hacienda Guayabal outside of Manizales, Villa Martha near Pereira, and Finca El Ocaso in Salento. Meanwhile, Hacienda Venecia has something for travelers of all budgets.

For bird-watchers, the lush region offers many parks and gardens to marvel at the hundreds of species in the area. The Reserva del Río Blanco near Manizales, Jardín Botánico del Quindío near Armenia, and the Santuario de Flora y Fauna Otún-Quimbaya near Pereira are within minutes of the city, guided walks are regularly offered, and birdlife is abundant. Outside of metropolitan areas, the Parque Municipal Natural Planes de San Rafael, which adjoins the Parque Nacional Natural Tatamá, is less known, but is a natural paradise.

Day trips to natural parks, including the Parque Nacional Natural Los Nevados, are easily organized. PNN Los Nevados is home to *páramos* (highland moors), lunar landscapes, and snow-capped volcanoes. It can be accessed from many points, and it can even be visited by car. Multiple day treks offer challenges.

If there were a Cute Pueblo Region of Colombia, this might be it. While you'll have more flexibility driving your own vehicle, it's easy to check out a pueblo or two from the region's major cities traveling by public transportation. A night or two is enough to experience the village life.

MANIZALES

The capital of the Caldas department, Manizales (pop. 393,200) is the region's mountain city. Instead of developing in a lowland valley like Armenia or Pereira, Manizales is set atop meandering mountain ridges. This location means that getting around town involves huffing and puffing up and down hills on foot, enduring rollercoaster-like bus or taxi rides along curvy roads, or taking the scenic route on the city's expanding Cable Aereo cable car network.

Above the coffee farms below at a higher altitude of 2,160 meters (7,085 feet), in Manizales good views abound. And any self-respecting sight around town has got to have a *mirador* (scenic lookout). On a clear day you can see the peaks of the Parque Nacional Natural Los Nevados in the distance, and this city serves as an excellent base to discover that rugged park of snowcapped volcanoes.

Visitors will keep busy here with many easily organized day-trip possibilities to coffee farms and natural parks. While in other cities dusk is a down time, when visitors return to their hotels or go online, in Manizales this is a good time to head out: to soak in a hot spring, to stroll the promenade along the Avenida 12 de Octubre and await a sunset, or to hang out in the Juan Valdez Café by the Torre del Cable.

ORIENTATION

The two main drags in Manizales—Avenida Santander (Carrera 23) and the Paralela (Carrera 25)—will take you to where you want to go in town.

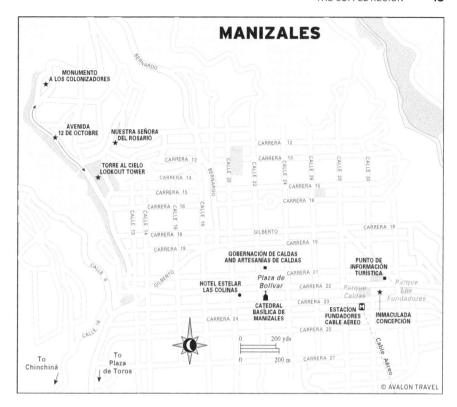

MANIZALES

They connect the Zona Rosa/El Cable area with downtown and with the Avenida 12 de October, which leads to Chipre and the Monumento a los Colonizadores.

Sights

As in all the major cities in the region, the real sights are in the tropical jungles. Manizaleños can be envied for having tropical forests at their backdoor. Here you can visit a park, feel like you're far away in the jungles of Colombia, but still be within the city limits. Birds, such as the colorful *barranquero* (blue-crowned motmot; the unofficial bird of Manizales) and many varieties of trees and flowers abound. Just outside of Manizales are coffee haciendas, parks, and gardens, all easily

visited from the city. In town, one day should suffice to see the urban attractions.

CENTRO

Downtown Manizales is bustling with activity during weekdays but vacates in a hurry in the evenings. There aren't many sights of interest, save for some republican period architecture and some noteworthy churches. Go on a weekend day if you can.

The Plaza de Bolívar (Cras. 21-22) holds an odd sculpture to honor Simón Bolívar created by Antioqueño Rodrigo Arenas Betancourt. It's known as the *Condor-Bolívar,* portraying the Liberator with a body of a condor, the national bird.

© ANDREW DIER

Manizales is Colombia's coffee capital.

Facing the plaza, the neo-gothic Catedral Basílica de Manizales (Cra. 22 No. 22-15, tel. 6/883-1880, open until 6:30pm daily) is imposing. Construction began in the late 1920s and was completed in 1936. It replaced the previous cathedral on the same spot, which had been damaged by earthquakes and had to be demolished. For 360-degree views of Manizales and beyond, climb around 500 steps up the spiral Corredor Polaco (the Polish corridor) in Colombia's tallest church tower. To climb the tower, you'll need a guide (COP$7,000). The tower is open 9am-noon and 2pm-5pm Thursday-Sunday.

Not as grandiose as the cathedral a couple of blocks away, the interior of the Inmaculada Concepción (Cl. 30 at Cra. 22, in the Parque Caldas, tel. 6/883-5474, 7am-noon and 2pm-6:30pm daily) is much more beautiful. The neo-gothic-style church, completed in 1909, was built with *bahareque* and *guadua,* natural materials used in construction across Colombia.

The wooden rib vaulted ceiling is made of cedar, as are the columns and pews.

CHIPRE

This neighborhood to the west of downtown is known for its views and sunsets. Manizaleños like to boast how Chilean poet Pablo Neruda, when strolling on the promenade in Chipre along the Avenida 12 de Octubre, marveled at this "sunset factory." Atop the futuristic lookout tower, La Torre al Cielo (10am-7pm Tues.-Sun., COP$2,000) you're guaranteed a nice vista.

At the far end of the walkway is the Monumento a los Colonizadores (Av. 12 de Octubre and Cra. 9, tel. 6/872-0420, ext. 22, 10am-6pm daily, free), designed by Luis Guillermo Vallejo. This monument honors the courage and sacrifice of Antioquian colonizers who settled the city, and it depicts an Antioquian family on horseback and on foot forging ahead, with cattle in tow, to this part of Colombia during the *colonización antioqueña,* when hundreds of families migrated

© ANDREW DIER

El Cable is a remnant of a gondola system that transported coffee over the Central Cordillera Mountains.

from Medellín to settle farms in the coffee region area. Manizales residents played a role in building the monument by donating keys and the like to be melted and used in its construction. The sculpture stands atop 20 tons of *piedra de mani* (peanut stone), the namesake for the city. It was inaugurated in 2001. To get to this part of the city, look for a bus with a "Chipre" sign along Avenida Santander (Cra. 23).

EL CABLE

One of the city's icons is a soaring wooden tower known as El Cable (52 meters/171 feet tall) that once supported the unusual gondola system that transported coffee (10 tons per hour!), other materials, and sometimes people from Manizales over the Central Cordillera. The system reached elevations of 3,700 meters (12,100 feet) and descended to the town of Mariquita (495 meters/1,625 feet). From there the coffee would be transported overland to Honda on the banks of the Río Magdalena.

The rest of the journey in Colombia would take the coffee north to the port city of Barranquilla, where it would be transferred to big boats bound for North America and Europe. This system was developed in the 1920s and would last until the early 1960s.

Of the 376 towers that supported the line, this particular tower, which was in the town of Herveo, was the only one built out of wood (all the others were made of iron). They were all supposed to be made of iron, but the boat carrying one of them from Europe to Colombia was sunk by a German submarine in the Atlantic Ocean during World War I. An English engineer in Colombia, who also designed the neat Estación del Cable, the adjacent station for the cable transport system, designed this tower using wood found locally. The Estación del Cable, a historic building, appropriately today houses the architecture department for the Universidad Nacional.

RESERVA DEL RÍO BLANCO

An array of birds, some found only in Colombia, can be spotted during an excursion to the Reserva del Río Blanco (Vereda Las Palomas, tel. 6/870-3810, cell tel. 310/422-1883, www.fundegar.com, 6am-6pm daily), only three kilometers (two miles) outside of Manizales. Most hostels can arrange this day trip, charging COP$20,000 per person for a guided group hike to strategic places in the jungle apt for spotting birds. Toucans and antpittas can often be seen, but over 362 species have been identified throughout the reserve. From August until March the area receives many migratory birds from North America. Private and longer bird-watching tours are also possible.

An *oso andino* (Andean bear) that lived in captivity for most of his life was adopted and now lives in an enclosed field in the reserve near the cabins. It was decided that he would not be able to be released back into the wild.

There are comfortable lodging options available in the park in two cabins (tel. 6/870-3810, cell tel. 310/422-1883, US$55 pp all meals) that have a total of eight rooms. These are specifically for bird-watchers. Birding guides are offered for the additional cost of US$60 for a Spanish-speaking guide and US$90 for a guide who speaks English. The porch of the lodge is an excellent place to commune with hummingbirds, who are regular customers at the hummingbird feeders.

Taxi transportation to the reserve costs COP$25,000 from Manizales.

RECINTO DEL PENSAMIENTO

For a walk in the park, the Recinto del Pensamiento (Km. 11 Vía al Magdalena, tel. 6/874-4157, www.recintodelpensamiento.com, COP$3,000) is a tranquil green space with guided nature walks, a chair lift (COP$17,000), a two-hectare orchid forest with 12,000 orchids, and a butterfly farm. The centerpiece of the park is the Pabellón de Madera, a large open-air event space made of *guadua* (a type of bamboo) built by a renowned Colombian architect, Simón Vélez.

ECOPARQUE LOS YARUMOS

On undisturbed mountainsides throughout Colombia, you have undoubtedly noticed the silvery-white leaves of the *yarumo blanco* tree. Should you get a closer look, you'll see that the leaves of this tree are actually green; it's a fuzzy layer on them that makes them appear white. The Ecoparque Los Yarumos (Cl. 61B No. 15A-01, Barrio Toscana, tel. 6/872-0420 ext. 22, 9am-6pm Tues.-Sun., free) is named for those deceptive trees. A few *yarumos* can be seen in the more than 50 hectares (125 acres) of cloud forest jungle that makes up this park. The park has nature paths, a lookout tower, and activities such as jungle zip lines. To get to the park on public transportation, you can take a bus from the Manizales city center bound for Minitas. It's about a 7- to 10-minute walk from the bus stop to the park entrance. Taxis are also cheap, costing under COP$4,000 from the El Cable area.

HOT SPRINGS

Near Manizales are two popular *termales* (hot springs). Bring your own towel and sandals for both, and visit on a weekday if you want to avoid the crowds.

Near a river, Tierra Viva (Km. 2 Vía Enea-Gallinazo, tel. 6/874-3089, www.termalestierraviva.com, 9am-midnight Mon.-Thurs., 9am-1am Fri.-Sun., COP$12,000-14,000) is closest to Manizales and less expensive. It consists of one pool, some bare-bones changing rooms, and a snack bar.

Considered the better and hotter of the springs, Termales Otoño (Km. 5 Vía Antigua El Nevado del Ruiz, tel. 6/874-0280, http://termaleselotono.com, 7am-midnight daily, day pass COP$25,000, COP$107,000-356,000 d) is a hot spring hotel complex a 25-minute ride to the southeast of the city. It's larger, with four pools (though two of these are reserved exclusively for hotel guests).

Festivals and Events

The Plaza de Toros (Cra. 27 10A-07, tel. 6/883-8124, www.cormanizales.com), or bullfighting ring, takes center stage every year at Manizales's biggest bacchanal, the Feria de Manizales (www.feriademanizales.gov.co), a celebration of the city's founding. During the festivities there are also concerts, a ballad festival (Festival de Trova), and a Miss Coffee beauty pageant. This citywide party is held in early January.

The theater festival in Bogotá, held every two years, is the most important theatrical event in Colombia. In second place is the annual Festival Internacional de Teatro de Manizales (www.festivaldemanizales.com). It's always held during the first week of September and attracts theater troupes primarily from the Americas. In addition to performances in theaters throughout the city, free performances are given in parks and plazas, and an educational program for aspiring young actors takes place in schools.

Shopping

Two popular shopping malls with inexpensive food options, movie theaters, and numerous clothing and other shops are Fundadores (Cl. 33B No. 20-03, tel. 6/889-4318, www.centrocomercialfundadores.com, 9am-9pm daily) and Cable Plaza (Cra. 23 No. 65-11, tel. 6/875-6595, 9am-9pm daily).

For handicrafts, peruse the locally made wares such as woodcarvings and woven items at the Artesanías de Caldas (Plaza de Bolívar, Gobernación de Caldas, Cra. 21 and Clls. 22-23, tel. 6/873-5001, www.artesaniasdecaldas.com, 8am-noon and 2pm-6pm Mon.-Sat.) downtown.

Sports and Recreation

The Ciclovía in Manizales takes place every Sunday from 8am to noon along the Avenida Santander (Carrera 23) and other main streets. The last Thursday of each month a Ciclovía Nocturna (7pm-10pm) is held. It's the nighttime version of the Ciclovía.

Once Caldas (www.oncecaldas.com.co) is the Manizales soccer club, and their stadium, the Estadio Palogrande (Cra. 25 No. 65-00) is in the Zona Rosa, within walking distance from many hostels and hotels. Once Caldas won the Copa Libertadores de America in 2004, defeating Boca Juniors from Buenos Aires, which was a big deal around these parts. Tickets can be purchased in the Cable Plaza Mall (Cra. 23 No. 65-11, tel. 6/875-6595, 9am-9pm daily).

Accommodations

The El Cable area in Manizales is the best place to stay, due to a large number of lodging options and its proximity to restaurants and shopping centers. It's a quiet neighborhood, bustling with international visitors, particularly on Calle 66. There is little traffic on streets here, which is nice; however, that often means that vehicles of all sorts zoom by at high speeds.

One of the long-standing budget accommodations in Manizales is Mountain Hostels (Cl. 66 No. 23B-91, tel. 6/887-4736, cell tel. 300/521-6120, www.mountainhostels.com.co, COP$22,000 dorm,

COP$60,000 d). Spread over two houses, it has a variety of room types and a small restaurant where you can order a healthy breakfast. Rooms aren't fancy, however.

Hostal Kumanday (Cl. 66 No. 23B-40, tel. 6/887-2682, cell tel. 315/590-7294, www.kumanday.com, COP$25,000 dorm, COP$40,000 pp d) is a quiet and clean option on the same street as Mountain Hostels. There are 10 rooms and one small dorm room, and all options include breakfast (but no fruit). Staff are a little shy. Kumanday has its own, highly recommended, tour agency that specializes in hiking in and around the Parque Nacional Natural Los Nevados. They also offer a downhill mountain-bike trip (COP$125,000 day trip, 3-person minimum) in the park.

Casa Lassio Hostal (Cl. 66 No. 23B-56, tel. 6/887-6056, cell tel. 310/443-8917, COP$23,000 dorm, COP$35,000 private room pp) has six rooms, and they also organize bike tours.

The Colombian chain Estelar (www.hotelesestelar.com) has three hotels in the Manizales area. They are among the top hotels in the city, and all have spacious and clean rooms, as well as at least one room that is accessible for people with disabilities. Weekend rates tend to be significantly lower than during the week. There are few reasons for wanting to stay in downtown Manizales, but if you do, Hotel Estelar Las Colinas (Cra. 22 No. 20-20, tel. 6/884-2009, COP$188,080 d) is the best option (but only on weekends, when traffic, noise, and general urban stress is manageable). The hotel's 60-some rooms are large and clean, but the restaurant and bar area is a little gloomy. A breakfast buffet is available for an additional cost.

The ◖ Estelar El Cable (Cra. 23C No. 64A-60, tel. 6/887-9690, COP$294,000 d) has 46 rooms over nine floors and is the upscale option in the El Cable/Zona Rosa area. Breakfast and a light dinner are often included in room rates. Rooms are spacious and clean, with pressed wood floors. A small gym offers modern cardio machines.

If you prefer birds and trees, check out Estelar's 32-room hotel at the Recinto del Pensamiento

(Km. 11 Vía al Magdalena, tel. 6/889-7077, COP$210,000 d). Outside the city, surrounded by nature, this hotel feels a little isolated. It's a popular place for business conferences and events during the week. Rooms are spacious.

Food

For excellent down-home, regional cuisine, head to Don Juaco (Cl. 65 No. 23A-44, tel. 6/885-0610, cell tel. 310/830-2218, noon-10pm daily, COP$15,000), which has been serving contented diners for decades. Try the Paisa hamburger: a hamburger sandwiched in between two arepas (cornmeal cakes). Enjoy it or the popular set lunch meals on the pleasant terrace.

For delectable grilled meat dishes, Palogrande (Cra. 23C No. 64-18, tel. 6/885-3177, 11am-10pm daily, COP$25,000) is the place you want. Located on a quiet street, it's a rather elegant, open-air place with a nice atmosphere.

For Italian fare, there are two decent options. Try Spago (Cl. 59 No. 24A-10, Local 1, tel. 6/885-3328, cell tel. 321/712-3860, noon-3pm and 6pm-10pm Mon.-Sat., noon-3pm Sun., COP$25,000), which is one of the upmarket restaurants in town, with tasty thin-crust pizzas. Il Forno (Cra. 23 No. 73-86, tel. 6/886-8515, noon-10pm Mon.-Sat., noon-3pm Sun., COP$22,000) is a family-style chain restaurant with a great view of the city.

Vegetarian restaurants exist in Manizales, but it's difficult to track them down. Orellana (Cl. 50 No. 26-40, tel. 6/885-3907, noon-3pm Mon.-Sat., COP$10,000) serves healthy set lunches and is located in the Versalles neighborhood. It's near the supermarket Confamiliares de la 50. Rushi (Cra. 23C No. 62-73, tel. 6/881-0326, cell tel. 310/538-8387, 11am-9pm Mon.-Sat., 11am-3pm Sun., COP$12,000) is a vegetarian restaurant close to the Zona Rosa area. It offers set lunches and á la carte dishes such as paella and vegetarian fried rice.

In Colombia, you are never far from a bakery selling sweets. In Manizales there is one bakery where you can have your sweets without the guilt. At Cero Azúcar (Cra. 23C No. 62-42, tel. 6/881-0625, 8:30am-8pm daily), all their cakes, cookies, and ice creams are made with the natural sweetener stevia.

A fantastic place for a late afternoon cappuccino and snack is Juan Valdez Café (Cra. 23B No. 64-55, tel. 6/885-9172, 10am-9pm daily). Yes, it's a chain, and there's one in any self-respecting mall in Colombia. But this one is different: Locals proudly boast that it is the largest Juan Valdez on the planet. But what truly sets this one apart is its great location, under the shadow of the huge wooden tower that once supported the coffee cable car line that ran from Manizales to Mariquita.

Information and Services

A Punto de Información Turística (Cra. 22 at Cl. 31, tel. 6/873-3901, 7am-7pm daily) can be of assistance in organizing excursions to parks and coffee farms throughout Caldas. The staff are eager to help. A small tourist office is also located in the main hall of the Terminal de Transportes (Cra. 43 No. 65-100).

In case of an emergency, Manizales has a single emergency line: 123. To speak directly with the police, call 112.

Getting There and Around

Avianca (Cra. 23 No. 62-16, Local 110, tel. 6/886-3137, www.avianca.com, 8am-6:30pm Mon.-Fri., 8am-1pm Sat.) and ADA (airport tel. 6/874-6332, 5:45am-5:45pm Mon.-Fri., 8am-5:30pm Sat., 3pm-5:30pm Sun.) serve Aeropuerto La Nubia (tel. 6/874-5451), about 10 kilometers (six miles) southeast of downtown. But the runway is often shrouded in clouds. Because of this, the airport is closed 35 percent of the time and always at night.

There is regular and speedy bus service to both Armenia (COP$17,500, 2 hours) and Pereira (COP$11,000, 70 mins.). Arauca (www.empresaarauca.com.co) runs buses to Pereira every 15 minutes and is considered a good company. Buses bound for Cali and Medellín cost around COP$35,000-40,000 and take five hours each. Buses to Bogotá cost COP$47,000 and take about nine hours.

The Terminal de Transportes (Cra. 43 No.

65-100, tel. 6/878-5641, www.terminaldemanizales. com) is spacious, orderly, and clean. From there it is about a 15-minute taxi ride to the Zona Rosa area. The terminal adjoins the cable car Cable Aereo station. The cable car route transports passengers from the terminal (Estación Cambulos) to the Fundadores station (Cra. 23 between Clls. 31-32) in the Centro.

Public transportation is not the most organized in Manizales. Private buses are easy to use, but you'll probably have to ask someone for help to determine which bus to flag down. To get downtown from the Zona Rosa, take a bus bound for Chipre.

Taxicabs are also plentiful. Guillermo Ortíz (cell tel. 313/766-8376) is highly recommended. Reliable cab companies include Taxi La Feria (tel. 6/884-8888), Taxi Ya (tel. 6/878-0000), and Taxi Express (tel. 6/880-2000). Many hotels and hostels routinely work with one or two specific taxi drivers, but if not, they will always order a cab for you.

Walking from the Zona Rosa area, along the Avenida Santander, to downtown will take about 45 minutes.

COFFEE FARMS

The Caldas countryside is home to coffee haciendas, large and small. Hacienda Venecia and Hacienda Guayabal are two of the most highly recommended for coffee tours, as well as overnight stays. They are located near Chinchiná, only a 30-minute drive from Manizales.

Hacienda Venecia

One of the most well-known, organized, and most visited coffee farms is Hacienda Venecia (Vereda El Rosario, Vía a Chinchiná, cell tel. 320/636-5719, www.haciendavenecia.com, coffee tour COP$35,000, COP$70,000-250,000 d). This large working coffee plantation has been in the same family for four generations, and their coffee was the first in Colombia to receive UTZ certification for sustainable farming, in 2002. The farm is set far from the highway, providing a peaceful atmosphere. When you're there, you're surrounded by coffee plants growing everywhere you look.

If you are day-tripping, organizing an excursion to the farm for a coffee tour is easy from Manizales. In fact, you won't have to do much at all except inform the hostel or hotel where you are staying that you'd like to go. The Hacienda Venecia makes a daily pickup at the main hostels in town at around 9am.

Tours are given at 9:30am with an additional tour offered at 2:30pm, depending on demand. The 2.5-hour tour begins with a comprehensive presentation of coffee-growing in Colombia and in the world, the many different aromas of coffee, and how to differentiate between a good bean and a bad bean. (And you'll be offered a knock-your-socks-off espresso to boot.) Later, the tour heads outside through the plantation, where you'll see coffee plants at all stages in the growing process. You'll also be able to observe the soaking and drying process. At the end, in the lovely original hacienda house, it's time to roast some beans and drink another freshly roasted cup of Venecia coffee. A typical lunch, such as *ajiaco* (chicken and potato soup), is offered as well (COP$10,000) at the end of the tour. A farm tour by Jeep and private tours (both COP$50,000) can also be arranged.

There are lodging options suitable for all budgets at Venecia. In the hostel, often a lively center of activity, accommodations are basic (and bathrooms are shared) but comfortable. For more luxury and seclusion, you may want to stay at the old hacienda house.

Other activities at the farm include horseback riding (for an additional fee) or walks around the plantation on your own. This is particularly pleasant to do early in the morning, when birds (more than 116 species!) are chirping.

Hacienda Guayabal

Near Venecia, Hacienda Guayabal (Km. 3 Vía Chinchiná-Pereira, cell tel. 314/772-4895, www.haciendaguayabal.com, tour COP$30,000, COP$95,000 pp all meals) has a dramatic setting, with mountains and valleys covered in coffee crops and *guadua* (bamboo) completely enveloping the hacienda. This is indeed a coffee farm, and one of the pioneers in coffee farm tourism, but equally interesting is to take a nature walk through the *guaduales* (forests of Colombia's bamboo) that always spring up along water sources. This hacienda has been in Doña María Teresa's family for around 50 years.

If you come, you might as well stay, so that you can enjoy the peace and warm hospitality of this special place. While accommodations in the six rooms are not luxurious, they are more than adequate. Meals are delicious, one of the things for which Guayabal is known. Tours around the *finca* (farm) take about two hours, and you learn about the coffee process as you maneuver along the rows of orderly coffee plants. In addition, you can hike up to a spectacular lookout on a mountainside for breathtaking views of the hills, the valleys, the forests, and the farms all around. Near the guesthouse is a hut made from *guadua* with recycled floor tiles that has a small coffee bar where you can have a cup of coffee and wait for birds of every color and shape to fly up to nibble on a piece of banana. Tranquility is the watchword here; it's no wonder Guayabal is occasionally host to meditation retreats.

◖ SALAMINA

Designated as one of Colombia's most beautiful pueblos, Salamina features history, beauty, personality, and spectacular countryside; yet, for the most part, it remains off of most tourists' radar. When you visit this historic town, you'll feel as if you have stumbled upon a hidden gem. The historic center of Salamina is marked by colorful and well-preserved two-story houses with their stunning woodwork, doors, and balconies. Salamina is often called the *pueblo madre* (mother town), as it was one of the first settlements of the Antioquian colonization. It's older than Manizales.

Sights

The Plaza de Bolívar (Clls. 4-5 between Cras. 6-7) is the center of activity in Salamina. It's an attractive plaza with a gazebo and large fountain brought over from Germany. Carried by mules over the mountains from the coast, it took a year to

arrive, in several pieces, to its final destination. The Basílica Menor La Inmaculada Concepción (Cl. 4 between Cras. 6-7) has an unusual architecture. The single nave worship hall is rectangular and flat with wooden beams and no columns. The church was designed by an English architect, who is said to have modeled it on the First Temple in ancient Jerusalem.

The Casa Rodrigo Jiménez Mejía (Cl. 4 and Cra. 6) is the most photographed house in Salamina. The colors of this exceptionally preserved house were chosen in an interesting way. An owner of the house called kids from the town to gather in the plaza and to give the owner their proposal on what colors to use for the house's exterior. The winner was a four-year-old girl, who chose bright orange, yellow, and green.

The Casa de la Cultura (Cra. 6 No. 6-06, tel. 6/859-5016, 8am-noon and 2pm-5pm Mon.-Fri., free) displays photos of old Salamina. It's often a hub of activity. It's also known as the Casa del Diablo, and a jovial devil wood-carving above the door greets visitors as they enter.

For decades, the Cementerio San Esteban (Cra. 3 between Clls. 2-4, no phone), the town cemetery, was divided into three sections: one for the rich, one for the poor, and another for so-called "N.N." bodies (non-identified corpses, or "no names"). A wall was built to divide the rich from the poor, but it was knocked down at the behest of a priest in 1976. A skull and crossbones is displayed over the cemetery entrance. There is a small neo-gothic style chapel (open occasionally) on the grounds.

In the village of San Félix, 30 kilometers (19 miles) east of Salamina, you can hike through serene countryside and admire a forest of *palmas de cera* (wax palms) from the hills above. Afterwards, on the village plaza, ask at the stores for a refreshing *helado de salpicón* (ice cream made from chunks of fresh fruit in frozen watermelon juice). A bus makes the round-trip (COP$10,000 each way) to San Felix twice a day, once in the early morning and again in the afternoon. It leaves from the plaza.

a friendly devil in Salamina

Festivals and Events

Salamina's Semana Santa (Holy Week) celebrations, which fall in either March or April, are not that well known, but it is, nonetheless, a great time to get to know this cute town. Orchids and other flowers adorn the balconies of houses, adding even more color. In addition, free classical, religious, and jazz music concerts are held in churches, plazas, and even the cemetery.

San Felix is known for its Exposición de Ganado Normando in July, when local farmers show off their best Norman cows, with various competitions. It's an important event for ranchers throughout the region, and also a chance to see an authentic display of Paisa culture.

Halloween is a big deal in Salamina. Here it's called the Tarde de María La Parda, named after a local woman who is said to have sold her soul to the devil in order to obtain riches. Her ghost supposedly causes mischief in the countryside every now and then. Events for Tarde de María La Parda take place in Plaza de Bolívar, and there are costume parties at night on that day.

December 7 is a special day—or rather, night—to be in Salamina. That's when the lights are turned off in Salamina, and the streets and balconies are illuminated with handmade lanterns made by locals. This beautiful celebration is called the Noche de las Luces, a night to stroll the streets and enjoy the special atmosphere. Locals greet each other serving sweets, snacks, or drinks. Music fills the air and the evening culminates in a fireworks show.

Accommodations

The best place to stay in Salamina by a long shot is the **C** Casa de Lola García (Cl. 6 No. 7-54, tel. 6/859-5919, www.lacasadelolagarcia. com, COP$120,000 d), which opened its doors in 2012. The dream of a native Salamineño, musician Mauricio Cardona García, the carefully restored house was once the home of his

a campesino near Salamina

grandmother, Lola García. Rooms are spacious and comfortable. If you provide Mauricio with some notice, meals at the hotel can be arranged.

Two other hotels in town, while not fancy, will do the trick if you're sticking to a budget. Hospedaje Casa Real (Cra. 6A No. 5-33, tel. 6/859-6355, cell tel. 311/784-2364, www.hospedajecasareal.wix.com, COP$50,000-80,000 d) has 24 rooms and is around the corner from the Plaza de Bolívar. The owners also have a *finca* with lodging facilities in the countryside. Hotel Colonial (Cl. 5 No. 6-74, tel. 6/859-5078, cell tel. 314/627-9124, hotelcolonial2011@hotmail.com, COP$35,000-50,000 d) is right on the square and has a variety of room options. In both of these hotels, ask to see the rooms before you check in, as their characteristics vary.

Based in Manizales, the travel agency Rosa de los Vientos (Centro Comercial Parque Caldas Nivel 2, Local PB45, tel. 6/883-5940, www.turismorosadelosvientos.com) can arrange a home stay (COP$25,000-35,000 pp) in one of the many historic homes in Salamina. The owner, Jackeline

Rendón, is from Salamina, knows the owners well, and will match you with a good fit.

Food

Popular and atmospheric Tierra Paisa (no phone, 8am-9pm daily, COP$7,000), below the Hotel Colonial on the park, serves typical Colombian food, like *bandeja paisa* (a quintessential Paisa dish of beans, various meats, yuca, and potatoes), at incredibly low prices.

You can't leave Salamina without trying their specialties. One is *macana,* a hot drink made of milk, ground up cookies, cinnamon, and sugar. The other is *huevos al vapor,* a boiled egg that is methodically steamed using giant coffee urns and served in a coffee cup. For the quintessential Salamina breakfast, go for both.

Getting There and Around

There is frequent shared taxi service to Salamina from Manizales, costing (COP$11,000). These depart from the Terminal de Transportes (Cra. 43 No. 65-100) in Manizales.

One bus leaves Medellín at 7am daily bound for Salamina and other communities in the area. It departs from the Terminal del Sur (Cra. 65 No. 8B-91, tel. 4/444-8020 or 4/361-1186). The trip takes 4-6 hours on rural roads.

◖ PARQUE NACIONAL NATURAL LOS NEVADOS

This national park covers 583 square kilometers (225 miles) of rugged terrain along the Central Cordillera between the cities of Manizales to the north, Ibagué to the southeast, and Pereira to the northwest. Whether you do a day trip or a multi-day trek, a visit to Parque Nacional Natural Los Nevados (www.parquesnacionales.gov.co) allows you to enjoy first-hand the stark beauty of the upper reaches of the Andes, far above the forest line, with its intriguing vegetation and fauna. Within the park are three snowcapped volcanoes, Nevado del Ruiz (5,325 meters/17,470 feet), Nevado del Tolima (5,215 meters/17,110 feet), and Nevado Santa Isabel (4,950 meters/16,240 feet), as well as myriad lakes, such as the Laguna del Otún.

This rugged landscape was formed by volcanic activity and later sculpted by huge masses of glaciers. At their maximum extension, these glaciers covered an area of 860 square kilometers (332 square miles). They began to recede 14,000 years ago and, according to a 2013 study by the Colombian Institute of Hydrology, Meteorology, and Environmental Studies (IDEAM), will completely disappear by 2030.

Most of the park consists of *páramo*, a unique tropical high altitude ecosystem, and super *páramo*, rocky terrain above the *páramo* and below the snow line. *Páramo* is a highland tropical ecosystem that thrives where UV radiation is higher, oxygen is scarcer, and where temperatures vary considerably from daytime to nighttime, when the mercury falls below freezing. It is the kingdom of the eerily beautiful *frailejones*, plants with statuesque tall trunks and thick yellow-greenish leaves. Other *páramo* vegetation includes shrubs, grasses, and cushion plants (*cojines*). The super *páramo* has

a stark, moonlike landscape, with occasional dunes of volcanic ash. Though it's largely denuded of vegetation, bright yellow plants called *litamo real* and orange moss provide splashes of color. On a clear day, the views from the *páramo* or super *páramo* of the snowcapped volcanoes and lakes are simply stunning.

The black and white Andean condor, *vultur gryphus,* with its wingspan of up to three meters (10 feet), can sometimes be spotted gliding along the high cliffs in the park. While it is estimated that there are over 10,000 of the birds on the continent (mostly in Argentina), there are few remaining in Colombia. Some estimates report that by the mid-1980s, there were no more than 15 left in Colombia, due in large part to poaching by cattle ranchers. In an effort to boost their numbers in Colombia, a reintroduction program was initiated in the park (and in other parts of the country) in the 1990s in conjunction with the San Diego Zoo, where newborns were hatched. Today it is estimated that there are 200-300 condors soaring above Colombia's Andean highlands. Numbers of the endangered birds in Los Nevados range 8-15. Other fauna includes spectacled bears *(oso de anteojos),* tapirs, weasels, squirrels, bats, and many species of birds.

The Nevado del Tolima and Nevado del Ruiz volcanoes are considered active, with the Ruiz presenting more activity. In 1986 it erupted, melting the glacier, which in turn created a massive mudslide that engulfed the town of Armero, burying an estimated 20,000 of the town's 29,000 residents.

ORIENTATION

The Northern Sector of the park includes the Nevado del Ruiz, with its three craters (Arenales, La Piraña, and La Olleta), and extends south to the extinct Cisne volcano and Laguna Verde. This part can be accessed by vehicle.

The Southern Sector includes everything from the Nevado Santa Isabel south to the Quindío peak, as well as Nevado del Tolima. This area has fewer visitors as access is only by foot or by horse, from Manizales, Pereira, Salento, or Ibagué.

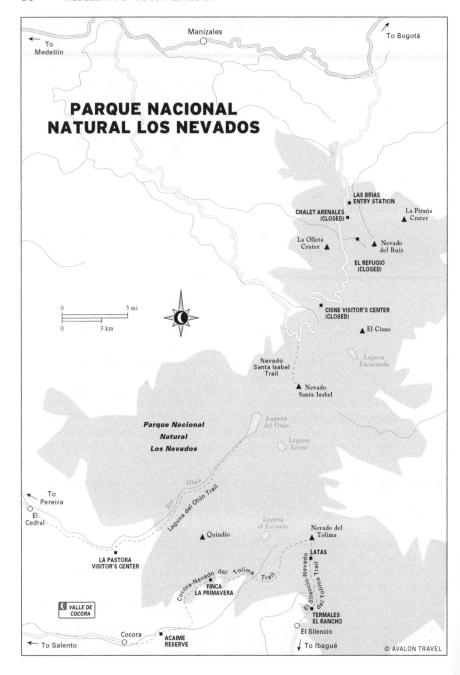

To Medellín

Manizales

To Bogotá

PARQUE NACIONAL NATURAL LOS NEVADOS

LAS BRIAS ENTRY STATION

CHALET ARENALES (CLOSED)

La Piraña Crater

La Olleta Crater

Nevado del Ruiz

EL REFUGIO (CLOSED)

0   3 mi

0   3 km

CISNE VISITOR'S CENTER (CLOSED)

El Cisne

Nevado Santa Isabel Trail

Laguna Encantada

Nevado Santa Isabel

Parque Nacional Natural Los Nevados

Laguna del Otún

Laguna Leona

To Pereira

El Cedral

Río Otún

Laguna del Otún Trail

Laguna el Encanto

Quindío

Nevado del Tolima

LATAS

LA PASTORA VISITOR'S CENTER

Cocora-Nevado del Tolima Trail

El Silencio-Nevado del Tolima Trail

VALLE DE COCORA

FINCA LA PRIMAVERA

TERMALES EL RANCHO

Cocora

ACAIME RESERVE

El Silencio

To Salento

To Ibagué

© AVALON TRAVEL

© ANDREW DIER

the lunar-like landscape of the Parque Nacional Natural Los Nevados

The Northern Sector

The Northern Sector (turnoff to Las Brisas entry point at Km. 43 Vía Manizales-Honda, tel. 6/887-1611, www.parquesnacionales.gov. co, 8am-2pm daily high season, COP$43,500 for nonresidents, COP$28,500 for residents, COP$24,500 for students with valid student ID, COP$5,000 per vehicle) is the most visited part of the park. Until recently, day trippers could drive from Manizales right up to El Refugio, a camp at the base of the Ruiz, and climb up to the main Arenales crater (5,325 meters/17,470 feet) in a strenuous three-hour hike. The Cisne visitors center provided lodging in this sector of the park and allowed easy access to the Nevado Santa Isabel and Laguna Verde.

Due to increased activity at Ruiz, the entire Northern Sector was closed from March 2012 through early 2013. In January 2013 a small area, from the Las Brisas entry station to the Valle de las Tumbas (also known as Valle del Silencio) was reopened to visitors in organized tours and private

vehicles. El Refugio at the base of the Ruiz, the Chalet Arenales camping site, and the Cisne visitors center are off limits. At the time of writing, there were no plans to reopen these facilities.

If you don't have a vehicle, the only way to visit this part of the park is on an organized day tour from Manizales. These tours leave at 6am, drive to Las Brisas park entry station, and continue on to the Valle de las Tumbas, making stops along the way to gaze at the landscape, particularly the Nevado del Ruiz and La Olleta crater (weather permitting), and to view birds and vegetation. On the way back to Manizales, the tour stops for an hour at the rundown Termales de Ruiz outside the park for a quick soak in warm sulfur-laden waters. The tours return to Manizales by 5pm. This experience will be unsatisfying for people who want to move their legs. Ecosistemas (Cra. 21 No. 23-21, Manizales, tel. 6/880-8300, www.ecosistema-stravel.com) offers this day tour for COP$100,000 for residents and COP$120,000 for nonresidents.

If you have a vehicle (a car with 4WD is not necessary) you can drive the Brisas-Valle de las Tumbas segment but you will be required to take a guide (included in the entry price) in your vehicle.

Another possibility to view Nevado del Ruiz without entering the park is to take an early morning milk truck (*lechero*) leaving Manizales at 5am to El Sifón, northeast of the park. The trip affords beautiful views of the *páramo* and the Ruiz in the distance and a chance to share a ride with farmers from the region. At El Sifón you can catch breakfast and walk back along the road to be picked up by the truck as it returns to Manizales, where you will arrive around noon. All the major hostels in Manizales know about how to organize this excursion.

The Southern Sector

The Southern Sector offers numerous trekking opportunities, several of which can be done without a guide. There are no official entry stations and permits are not required, but be prepared to pay an entry fee if you bump into a ranger. If you want to be meticulous, you can pay in advance by contacting the Parques Nacionales office in Bogotá (tel. 1/353-2400, www.parquesnacionales.gov.co), sending the names of the visitors to the park, depositing the entry fee at a bank, and receiving a permit by email. However, this is a huge hassle and very few people do it.

Nevado Santa Isabel Trek

A spectacular day trek from Manizales is up to the snow line of the Nevado Santa Isabel. It is a long day trip, starting with a bumpy 50-kilometer (31-mile) drive to the border of the park at Conejeras and then a three-hour (5.5-kilometer/3.4-mile) hike up the canyon of the Río Campo Alegre and then to the snow line. This hike requires good physical condition as it takes you from an elevation of 4,000 meters (13,100 feet) up to 4,750 meters (15,600 feet) through *páramo* and super *páramo*. More serious mountaineers can extend the trek to the summit of the Nevado Santa Isabel (4,950 meters/16,240 feet) by camping past Conejeras and doing an early morning ascent to the top. At sunrise, the views onto the surrounding high mountain landscape, with the Nevado del Ruiz and Nevado del Tolima in the background, are magnificent. The ascent to the top requires specialized gear.

There is no public transportation to Conejeras and the trails are not clearly marked, so an organized tour from Manizales is the way to go. A recommended tour operator is Kumanday (Cl. 66 No. 23B-40, Manizales, tel. 6/887-2682, cell tel. 315/590-7294, kumandaycolombia@gmail.com, www.kumanday.com). The folks at Mountain Hostels (Cl. 66 No. 23B-137, Manizales, tel. 6/887-4736, www.mountainhostels.com.co) can also help you organize this trek.

Laguna del Otún Trek

A popular three-day trek from Pereira is to the Laguna del Otún. The starting point is El Cedral, a *vereda* (village) 21 kilometers (13 miles) east of Pereira at an altitude of 2,100 meters (6,900 feet). The end point of the trek at the lake is at 3,950 meters (13,000 feet). This 19-kilometer (12-mile) hike provides an incredible close-up view of the transitions from humid tropical forest to higher altitude tropical forests and the *páramo*. The trek follows the valley of the crystalline Río Otún, first through the Parque Regional Natural Ucumarí and then into the Parque Nacional Natural Los Nevados. It's not too strenuous. Most trekkers split the climb into two segments, camping at El Bosque or Jordín on the way up and spending one night at the Laguna del Otún. The return hike can be done in one day. The path is easy to follow, though quite rocky and muddy. A guide is not necessary.

The only accommodation along this route is at the Centro de Visitantes La Pastora (6 km/4 mi from El Cedral toward Laguna del Otún, no phone, cell tel. 312/200-7711, COP$22,000 pp) in the Parque Regional Natural Ucumarí. The dormitory-style rooms are clean and comfortable in this cozy lodge. Meals (COP$6,000-9,000) by the fireplace are excellent. It is possible to buy snacks along the way, but there is no food at the *laguna,* so bring cooking equipment and food along with tents and sleeping bags.

To get to El Cedral from Pereira, take a *chiva* (rural bus) offered by Transportes Florida (tel. 6/331-0488, COP$5,000, 2 hrs.), which departs from Calle 12 and Carrera 9 in Pereira. On weekdays, the bus departs at 7am, 9am, and 3pm. On weekends there is an additional bus at noon. The buses return from El Cedral approximately at 11am, 2pm, and 5pm.

The Laguna del Otún can also be visited on an organized tour in a long day trip from Pereira. This involves leaving Pereira at 5am and driving 88 kilometers (55 miles) to Potosí (3,930 meters/12,895 feet) near the park border and then hiking two hours to the lake. This is not a strenuous walk. A recommended tour operator in Pereira for this excursion is Cattleya Ser (Cl. 99 No. 14-78, La Florida, cell tel. 314/642-6691 or 311/380-8126, www.cattleyaser.com.co). The Kolibrí Hostel (tel. 6/331-3955, cell tel. 321/646-9275, www.kolibrihostel.com) in Pereira also offers guided treks to the laguna.

Nevado del Tolima and Paramillo del Quindío Treks

There are two ways to reach the classically cone-shaped Nevado del Tolima (5,215 meters/17,110 feet). The somewhat easier and more scenic route is from Vereda del Cocora near Salento, which takes four days. A more strenuous route is up from El Silencio, near Ibagué, which can be done in two days.

From Vereda del Cocora (2,200 meters/7,215 feet), you hike 7-8 hours (13.5 kilometers/8.4 miles) through the Valle del Cocora, up the Río Quindío canyon, through the Páramo Romerales to the Finca La Primavera at 3,680 meters (12,075 feet). There you spend the night (COP$10,000 pp) and take a simple meal. On the second day you hike 6-7 hours (12 kilometers/7.5 miles) to a campsite at 4,400 meters (14,450 feet) near the edge of the super *páramo.* On the third day, you depart the campsite at 2am and climb a further 8 kilometers (5 miles) to reach the rim of the Tolima crater at 7 or 8am, when there are incredible views to the Quindío, Santa Isabel, Cisne, and Ruiz peaks. That evening you sleep again at the Finca La Primavera and return to Vereda del Cocora on the following day. The path is not clearly marked and it is easy to lose your way (there's a reason why one part is called the Valle de los Perdidos or Valley of the Lost!), so it is best go with a guide. The ascent to the glacier requires specialized gear.

From Ibagué the starting point for the trek to Nevado del Tolima is El Silencio, a small *vereda* (settlement) 28 kilometers (17 miles) north of the city at the end of the beautiful Río Combeima river canyon. From El Silencio, you'll walk 2.5 kilometers (1.5 miles) along a mountain path to El Rancho Tolima Termales (tel. 8/266-2152, cell tel. 310/817-2526, www.ranchotolimatermales. com, 24 hours daily, COP$5,000) hot springs. From there, there are several routes up to the top of Tolima. The most direct route is via La Cueva. It is a strenuous six- to eight-hour (15-kilometer/9-mile) hike up dense tropical forest, *páramo,* and super *páramo* to Latas, an unmarked camp spot

near some large rusting metal sheets. Water is available nearby.

From Latas, the ascent up the glacier to the rim of the volcano takes 3-4 hours and requires crampons and an ice axe. The return trip takes 5-6 hours, not including a soothing dip at the *termales.* Unless you are an experienced mountaineer, a guide is necessary.

Another less traveled but beautiful hike is to the Paramillo del Quindío (4,750 meters/15,585 feet), an extinct volcano that once was covered by a glacier. The 17-kilometer (10.5-mile) ascent from La Primavera Farm takes eight hours and can be done in one long day. Alternatively, you can split the hike in two, camping so as to arrive at the top of the crater in the early morning when visibility is best. There are spectacular views of the Tolima, Santa Isabel, and Ruiz volcanoes. This is a strenuous but not technically difficult climb.

Recommended guides for the Tolima and Quindío treks are Páramo Trek in Salento (cell tel. 311/745-3761, paramotrek@gmail.com) and Truman David Alfonso Bejarano in Ibagué (cell tel. 315/292-7395, trumandavid01@gmail. com), who can organize excursions from Salento or Ibagué. His blog (www.truman-adventure. blogspot.com) has detailed information about the various possible routes up to Nevado del Tolima.

Mountain Biking

There are many possible mountain-bike trips through the park, ranging from the easy (all downhill) to the fairly strenuous. Kumanday (Cl. 66 No. 23B-40, Manizales, tel. 6/887-2682, cell tel. 315/590-7294, kumandaycolombia@gmail.com, www.kumanday.com) offers several excursions.

ARMENIA

The defining moment for Colombia's Ciudad Milagro (Miracle City) arrived uninvited on the afternoon of January 25, 1999, when an earthquake registering 6.4 on the Richter scale shook the city. One thousand people lost their lives, nearly half the city became instantly displaced,

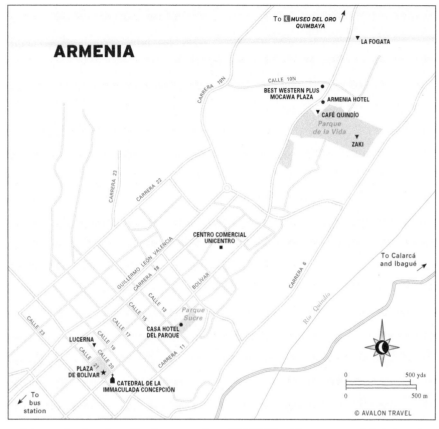

and thousands of nearby coffee farms were destroyed. The miracle of this coffee region city can be seen in how it rapidly rebuilt and began to thrive once more.

As is the case with sister cities Pereira and Manizales, Armenia was settled in the late 19th century by Antioquian colonizers. The city is not a tourist destination itself, but you'll be astonished to see, within just a few blocks of the city center, a sea of green coffee farms. That lush countryside is the real attraction.

The city was founded in 1889 and initially named Villa Holguín to honor then-president Carlos Holguín Mallarino. It is widely believed that the city was renamed Armenia to honor victims of the 1894-1896 Hamidian massacres of ethnic Armenians living in the Ottoman Empire.

ORIENTATION

Armenia is a small city by Colombian standards, home to 294,000 residents. Although there is not much to see or do downtown, it is a compact area, and it's easy to get around on foot. The northern areas of the city are where the hotels, malls, and restaurants are to be found. That part of town, around the Hotel Armenia, is also walkable.

Carreras run north-south and *calles* east-west. Main drags include Carreras 14 (Avenida Bolívar), 18, and 19, as well as the Avenida Centenario, which runs parallel to the Río Quindío on the eastern side of the city. Carrera 14 is pedestrian-only downtown.

Sights

Standing in downtown Armenia's Plaza de Bolívar (between Cras. 12-13 and Clls. 20-21) is a sculpture of Simón Bolívar (northern side of the plaza) and the love-it-or-hate-it Monumento al Esfuerzo, by Rodrigo Arenas Betancourt, built in the 1960s. This sculpture stands in remembrance of the sacrifices made and hardships faced by Antioquian settlers who arrived in the area seeking opportunity. The modern Catedral de la Inmaculada Concepción (Cra. 12 between Clls. 20-21, hours vary), completed in 1972, is a concrete, triangular-shaped building that replaced the previous cathedral, which had stood since 1927. The plaza is on the stark side.

A stroll down the pedestrian street from the Plaza de Bolívar to the Parque Sucre is a pleasant way to see the modern downtown at its busiest.

◖ MUSEO DEL ORO QUIMBAYA

Even if you have visited the world-famous Museo del Oro in Bogotá, it is worth the trek to Armenia just to visit the Museo del Oro Quimbaya (Av. Bolívar No. 40N-80, tel. 6/749-8433, www.banrepcultural.org, 10am-5pm Tues.-Sun., free) on the outskirts of town. In contrast to the Gold Museum in Bogotá, this museum, designed by famed architect Rogelio Salmona, focuses exclusively on the Quimbaya nation, which predominated in the coffee region before the Spanish conquest. Much of the museum is devoted to ceramic and gold decorative and ceremonial items that were found in the area. Excellent explanations in English provide interesting background information on the history, ways of life, and traditions of the Quimbaya people.

Festivals and Events

Armenios celebrate their city's founding in October with their Fiestas Cuyabras or Fiestas de Armenia. (People from Armenia are also called Cuyabras, after a bush that produced pumpkin-like fruit that was once widespread in the region.) City parks and plazas are the stages for cultural events, a beauty pageant, and a fun Yipao (Jeep) parade. These U.S. military Jeeps (called Jeep Willys), a symbol of the region, began arriving in Colombia around 1946, after World War II.

Recreation

Several city parks and plazas are great places to enjoy the delicious Armenia climate. These include the Parque de la Vida (Cra. 13 at Cl. 8N) and the Parque Sucre (Cra. 13 at Cl. 13) downtown, which is adjacent to a delightful pedestrian street. Locals and visitors gather in the late afternoon at the Café Quindío in the park for *onces* (tea time).

The Parque El Bosque (Cl. 21 No. 22-23) is a green space that has a bust of Abraham Lincoln that was donated to the city by the Armenian community of Fresno, California, as a way of expressing their gratitude for naming the city in solidarity with the decimated Armenian nation in the early 20th century. The bullfighting ring is in this park.

Globos Colombia (cell tel. 320/667-7818, www.globoscolombia.com, COP$390,000) offers commanding views of the Zona Cafetera from a hot-air balloon. Flights usually depart 6am-6:30am and last 45 minutes. A hearty Paisa breakfast is included in the tour. Flights depart from nearby Armenia as well as near Pereira, about an hour's drive away.

Shopping

The Centro Comercial Unicentro (Cra. 14 No. 6-02, tel. 6/731-2667, 8am-9pm daily) along the Avenida Bolívar has the usual array of Colombian mall stores, fast food joints, an Éxito department store, a movie theater, several ATMs, and food and coffee courts (with spectacular views of the bucolic valley). El Portal del Quindío (Av. Bolívar 19N No. 46-057, www.elportaldelquindio.com, 8am-9pm daily) is down the road from Unicentro and offers similar shops.

Accommodations

The Casa Quimbaya (Cl. 16N No. 14-92, tel. 6/732-3086, cell tel. 312/590-0066, www.

casaquimbaya.com, COP$20,000 dorm, COP$60,000 d) is the budget hostel option in Armenia. It is near the Universidad del Quindío. There are two dorm rooms and four private rooms. It's in an ordinary-looking house on a quiet street, very close to the action of Carrera 14.

A midrange option downtown is Casa Hotel del Parque (Cra. 14 No. 12-26, tel. 6/731-3166, www.casahoteldelparque.com, COP$99,000 d). It has five rooms and a great location on the Parque Sucre and the pedestrian street.

The Armenia Hotel (Av. Bolívar and Cl. 8N, tel. 6/746-0099, cell tel. 320/696-9111, www.armeniahotel.com.co, COP$220,000 d) has long been considered the most elegant place to stay in town. However, it has lost some of its panache over the years. It's got 129 rooms on nine floors, and a big atrium smells of eucalyptus emanating from the steam room. Rooms and bathrooms are spacious, the beds are fine, and you could go to town raiding the mini-bar. A spa, pool, and small gym are available on the premises, and guests also have privileges at a gym four blocks away.

The first U.S. hotel chain will soon be arriving in Armenia in the form of Best Western Plus Mocawa. It will have 97 rooms over 16 floors, a gym and spa, and a coffee bar in the lobby. Its location on the Avenida Bolívar is close to malls. It is scheduled to open in late 2013.

Food

Armenia's gastronomic center is uptown along Avenida Bolívar.

In the Centro, Lucerna (Cl. 20 No. 14-40, tel. 6/741-1005, 9am-7:30pm Mon.-Sat., 11am-6:30pm Sun.) is a classic. This retro-looking *salón de té* (tearoom) is always packed; you can order a meal or snack.

If you've got an appetite, head to La Fogata (Av. Bolívar No. 14N-39, tel. 6/749-5980, www.lafogata.com.co, noon-midnight daily, COP$28,000), a classic in Armenia. Their filet mignon is known as the best in town. Several Peruvian dishes make the menu interesting, and the loungey Café La Fogata is a popular place for a cocktail after work

or before a night out dancing. Nearby, the Café Quindío Gourmet (Parque de la Vida, Cra. 14/Av. Bolívar 7N, tel. 6/745-4478, www.cafequindio.com.co, 11am-9:30pm Mon.-Sat., noon-4:30pm Sun.) serves coffee drinks from Armenia's preferred coffee brand, Café Quindío, and more substantial meals such as pastas and sandwiches.

Practically hidden behind a residential complex near the Armenia Hotel, Zaki (Cra. 13 No. 8N-39, Edificio Bambú, Local 104, tel. 6/745-1220, noon-3pm and 6pm-10pm Mon.-Thurs., noon-3pm and 6pm-11pm Fri.-Sat., COP$20,000) is a sushi joint that also serves a mish-mash of other Asian-inspired dishes. It is one of a handful of restaurants and bars in this part of town that cater to Armenia yuppies.

Natural Food Plaza (Cra. 14 No. 4-51, tel. 6/745-1597, 7:30am-6pm Mon.-Thurs., 7:30am-4pm Fri. and Sun., COP$10,000) always has a set lunch, but you can also order Paisa dishes, like tamales and *bandeja paisa*—the quintessential Paisa dish of beans, various meats, yuca, and potatoes—reinvented vegetarian-style, all to the soothing sounds of elevator music.

Many of the best-known restaurants in Armenia are on the outskirts of town, like El Roble (Km. 12 Vía Armenia Pereira, tel. 6/740-5120, 6:30am-9pm daily, COP$15,000), which is a sprawling 100 percent Colombian cuisine family-style restaurant.

Information and Services

Tourist offices are located at the bus station (Cl. 35 No. 20-68) and in the Edificio de la Gobernación (Plaza de Bolívar, tel. 6/741-7700, 8am-noon and 2pm-6pm Mon.-Sat.).

Getting There and Around

Major airlines Avianca (Centro Comercial Portal del Quindío, Av. Bolívar No. 19N-46, 2nd floor, tel. 6/734-5205, www.avianca.com, 10:30am-1:30pm and 2:30pm-7:30pm Mon.-Sat., 11am-1:30pm and 2:30pm-7pm Sun.) and LAN (Col. toll-free tel. 01/800-094-9490, www.lan.com) as well as smaller Colombian carriers EasyFly (tel. 6/747-9031, www.easyfly.com.co) and Aerolíneas de Antioquia

(Col. toll-free tel. 01/800-051-4232 www.ada-aero.com) serve the Aeropuerto Internacional El Eden (Km. 10 Vía La Tebaida, tel. 6/747-9400). Spirit Air (www.spirit.com) has two weekly non-stop flights from Fort Lauderdale.

The bus terminal, the Terminal de Transportes (Cl. 35 No. 20-68, tel. 6/747-3355, www.terminalarmenia.com) is just south of downtown, about 13 blocks from the Plaza de Bolívar. There is frequent service to Pereira (1 hour, COP$8,000), Salento (1 hour, COP$4,000), and Manizales (4 hours, COP$17,000). Buses bound for Medellín (6.5 hours, COP$38,000) leave all day from before dawn to around midnight. While short-distance buses depart until about 10pm or later, it's better to travel earlier if possible out of safety reasons and in order to enjoy the scenery along the way.

The rapid bus system in Armenia is called the Tinto (www.tinto.com.co), after the ubiquitous little coffees. A line on Avenida Bolívar connects the northern part of the city with downtown. The website can be confusing, so it's best to ask someone how to get around.

VICINITY OF ARMENIA
C Jardín Botánico del Quindío

Just 10 minutes outside of town, the well-run Jardín Botánico del Quindío (Km. 3 Vía al Valle, tel. 6/742-7254, cell tel. 310/835-0236, www.jardinbotanicoquindio.org, 9am-4pm daily, English tour COP$30,000) is home to hundreds of tree and plant species, many of which are threatened. Knowledgeable volunteer guides, who are usually college students, lead visitors on a mandatory 2.5-hour tour along jungle paths, stopping every so often to point out flora that you would have overlooked had you walked through on your own. That might strike you as a major time commitment, but it really doesn't seem like it. In addition to palms (which aren't technically trees) and *guadua* (which is actually related to grass), look out for *matapalos,* a tree that wraps itself around other trees, strangling them as they fight for sunlight. It's

© ANDREW DIER

Jardín Botánico del Quindío

been lovingly nicknamed the *abrazo de la suegra* (mother-in-law's hug).

In Colombia where there is tropical forest, there will be birds. The gardens are no exception, and they are home to at least 119 species. The birds are at their most active early in the morning. Some of the commonly seen species include tanagers, toucans, owls, woodpeckers, the multi-colored *torito cabecirrojo* (red-headed barbet), and iconic *barranqueros* or *barranquillos* (blue-crowned motmots). These birds make their nests in the earth. Rodent residents who frequently make cameo appearances are *ardillas* (squirrels) and cute *guatines* (Central American agoutis). By far the most photographed sector of the park is the *mariposario* (enclosed butterfly garden) in the shape of a giant butterfly, home to thousands. This is an interactive experience, in which visitors are encouraged to coax the insects to light on their fingers, arms, and shoulders. Butterflies are livelier when the sun is out.

Guides are volunteers, and although the entry price is steep, it's good form to tip the guides after the tour. Call in advance to inquire about English-speaking tours.

It's easy to get to the park using public transportation from Armenia. Just look for a bus from the Plaza de Bolívar or along Avenida Bolívar that says "Jardín Botánico."

Theme Parks

These parks are always mobbed with Colombian families on weekends and holidays.

RECUCA (Km. 5 Vía La Y-Barcelona, Vereda Callelarga, tel. 6/749-8525, www.recuca.com, 9am-3pm daily, tour with lunch COP$30,000) is a theme park, but one without rollercoasters or water rides. RECUCA stands for Recorrido de la Cultura Cafetera (Coffee Culture Experience). Upon arrival at the *finca* (farm), you'll be greeted by smiling employees dressed in traditional bean-picking garb. Then you'll explore a coffee farm, lend a hand by picking some ripe beans, and learn about the whole process. After that, you'll enjoy a big Paisa lunch (beans and rice for herbivores). If you prefer, you can just take part in a coffee-tasting session

(COP$11,000). You can get to RECUCA by taking a bus bound for Barcelona from the Terminal de Transportes in Armenia (Cl. 35 No. 20-68). The bus drops you off at the park entrance. From there it is a 30-minute walk, or the guard at the entrance can order a Jeep for you (COP$5,000).

The Parque Nacional del Café (Km. 6 Vía Montenegro-Pueblo Tapao, tel. 6/741-7417, www.parquenacionaldelcafe.com, 9am-6pm daily, COP$22,000-55,000) is near the town of Montenegro, 12.5 kilometers (8 miles) west of Armenia. While part of the park is devoted to telling the story of coffee production in Colombia, it's mostly an amusement park with rollercoasters, a chair-lift ride, horseback rides, a coffee show, a water park, and other attractions.

PANACA (Km. 7 Vía Vereda Kerman, tel. 6/758-2830, cell tel. 313/721-9211, www.panaca.com.co, 9am-6pm daily, COP$30,000-60,000) is an agricultural-themed amusement park near the town of Quimbaya, where visitors can see and interact with all types of farm animals and watch the occasional pig race.

Festivals and Events

In June or sometimes July, Calarcá puts on an event to honor what made the coffee region what it is today. A number of the usual festival events take place during the Fiesta Nacional del Café (www.calarca.net), but it's the Desfile de Yipao that steals the show. That's when Jeep Willys—U.S. military Jeeps from World War II and the Korean War that were sold to farmers in the coffee region—are laden down with people, animals, and furniture, and go on parade. There are competitions (essentially Willy beauty pageants) and a contest in which the Jeep Willys are loaded down with 1,800 kilos of cargo and race forward on two wheels only. The ubiquitous Jeep Willy has become a symbol of the region.

Accommodations and Food

With more than a century's experience growing coffee, the Hacienda Combia (Km. 4 Vía al Valle-Vereda La Bella, tel. 6/746-8472, cell tel.

314/682-5395, www.combia.com.co, COP$153,000 d) produces Café Inspiración, their brand of high-quality coffee. It is operated by the same owners as the Hacienda San José near Pereira. It has around 30 rooms and an infinity pool that has a fantastic view, and there are coffee tours available through the nearby fields. This hotel is not far from a highway, but you can easily block out reminders of suburbia by focusing on the fertile lands that surround you and are home to colorful birds. Its proximity to the airport (airport pickups can be arranged) and easy access make it popular for events with Colombian businesses. It also attracts foreign embassy staff living in Bogotá.

Bakkho (Cl. 41 No. 27-56, Calarcá, tel. 6/743-3331, www.bakkho.com, noon-9pm Tues., noon-10pm Wed.-Sun., COP$35,000) is considered to be the top restaurant in Quindío. Here, presentation and ambience is everything, and it's no surprise that this is where locals come to celebrate special occasions. Fare is international with many seafood dishes. Bakkho has various locations in the area, but the Calarcá location is the original.

Surrounded by 160 hectares of pineapple, cacao, banana, and citrus crops, it's hard to imagine a more relaxing place than sublime ◖ Hacienda Bambusa (off Vía Calarcá-Caicedonia south of Armenia, tel. 6/740-4935, cell tel. 321/313-7315, www.haciendabambusa.com, COP$160,000 pp). Its isolation is a selling point, as you feel far from everything, providing the perfect environment to disconnect. The house and much of the furniture are made of *guadua* and other traditional materials, and rooms are luxurious and tastefully decorated. There are only seven rooms, each with a private balcony or terrace. The views from those balconies are spectacular, with endless farms punctuated by *guadua* forests and mountains in the distance. Meals are prepared by the acclaimed Bakkho restaurant. It is isolated here, and it would be a shame to spend the day rushing around the area sightseeing. Here at the farm there are cacao tours to take, horses to ride, birds to watch, and massages to be enjoyed. The Armenia airport is about 40 minutes away,

and taking a cab from there costs COP$45,000, although the hotel can arrange all your transportation. Bambusa offers a range of packages, some including activities and excursions, transportation to and from the airport, and all meals. They do not bump up prices during high season (nor reduce prices during low season).

Near the town of Quimbaya and off the road 800 meters past some ordinary looking houses and apartments, a spectacularly well-maintained red-and-white-painted hacienda awaits: ◖ Finca Villa Nora (tel. 6/741-5472, cell tel. 310/422-6335, www.quindiofincavillanora.com, COP$180,000 d with 2 meals). It's a 120-year-old house that is charming and full of character. It's built in the typical Paisa style. Amid fruit trees, flowers, coffee fields, and a huge ficus tree, at Villa Nora the air is pure, sunsets lovely, and drinks on the verandah not a bad idea. There are only seven rooms at this quiet refuge.

SALENTO

On the western edge of the Parque Nacional Natural Los Nevados, the pueblo of Salento (pop. 7,000) is one-stop shopping for those seeking a quintessential coffee region experience. The town, an enchanting pueblo, home to coffee growers and cowboys, is adorned with the trademark colorful balconies and facades of Paisa architecture. It was one of the first settlements in the region during the 19th-century Antioquian colonization. In the nearby countryside, coffee farms dominate the landscape. Here you can be a Juan Valdez, the iconic personification of Colombian coffee, during a coffee tour in which you harvest coffee beans, learn about the bean-to-bag process, and sip the freshest coffee you've ever tasted.

Within minutes of town is the Valle de Cocora, where you can play tree tag in forests of *palma de cera* (wax palm, the Colombian national tree), the skyscrapers of the palm family. Some of these can reach up to 60 meters (200 feet) high. For a more challenging hike continue on to the Reserva Acaime, a private nature reserve of tropical forest, babbling brooks, and not a few hummingbirds.

From here adventurers can ascend into the *páramos* (highland moors) and, eventually, the snowcapped mountains of the Parque Natural Nacional Los Nevados.

Salento is easily accessed from between both Armenia and Pereira, and in the town and nearby countryside there are hostels, hotels, and good restaurants. It is a popular tourist destination, so if you'd like to experience Salento without the crowds, go during the week.

Sights

The Plaza de Bolívar or Plaza Principal is the center of town and center of activity. The festive pedestrian Calle Real (between Cl. 1 and Cl. 5) is the most photogenic street in Salento. It is lined with restaurants and souvenir shops painted in a rainbow of colors. It starts at the Plaza Principal and leads up to the Alto de la Cruz Mirador (scenic lookout atop the Calle Real). At the cross you can get a great bird's-eye view of the Calle Real and Salento. Farther on is another lookout with views over the surrounding jungles and valleys. But it's really about atmosphere in this Quindío town.

Coffee Tours

In the outskirts of Salento, an excellent place to learn about the coffee process from seed to cup is the Finca El Ocaso (Vía Salento-Vereda Palestina, cell tel. 310/451-7329, cafeelocaso@hotmail.com, www.fincaelocasosalento.com, 8:30am-4:30pm daily, tour COP$8,000). This family-run farm with some 12 hectares (30 acres) of coffee crops produces coffee that has several international certifications, such as the German UTZ and the Rainforest Alliance. Elevation here is around 1,780 meters, a good altitude to grow coffee. Gregarious Don Elias and his wife, Gloria Luz, run the farm, and they enjoy showing their farm to visitors. It's a fairly interactive tour, lasting around 40 minutes, in which you plant a coffee seed, strap a basket to your hip to harvest some ripe, red beans, and grind the coffee pulp. Then, of course, you get to try a freshly roasted cup at the end. The *finca* (farm) also has three cozy

rooms (COP$35,000-100,000), decorated with period furniture, available for rent in the traditional coffee plantation house. You can also rent the whole house (COP$420,000). If you'd like a tour in English, it's best to give the owners some advance notice. It's about an hour-long walk from town, or you can hire a Jeep Willy.

You can also check out the Finca Don Eduardo coffee tour (Plantation House, Alto de Coronel, Cl. 7 No. 1-04, cell tel. 316/285-2603, COP$20,000). There are two daily, at 9am and 3pm. This organic *finca* is run by the folks from Plantation House.

Recreation

For the real Paisa experience, horseback riding is a good way to enjoy the countryside around Salento. In the Plaza Principal there are usually horses at the ready, especially on weekends. One popular excursion is to some nearby waterfalls. Don Álvaro (cell tel. 311/375-1534, 3-hr. trip COP$40,000 pp) treats his horses well and is considered the best guide for this activity.

Salento, along with the neighboring countryside, is a nice place for a bike ride. Most hostels can arrange bike rental. Additionally, CicloSalento (near Plantation Hostel, Alto de Coronel, Cl. 7 No. 1-04, cell tel. 318/872-9714, COP$10,000/hr., COP$35,000/day) rents out good quality mountain bikes with helmets. Caution: The winding road leading into town from the Valle de Cocora does not have a shoulder for bikes. Vehicles tend to speed along this road, making this a dangerous stretch for cyclists and pedestrians.

Accommodations

As Salento has grown in popularity, with Paisa weekenders and international travelers, excellent accommodations options (from backpacker lodges to coffee plantations and camping options) to fit all budget types have similarly grown. Although the number of higher-end hotels in town is growing, it is often the case that small hostels and nearby coffee farms will suit your needs just fine.

One of the best hostels in the area is ◖ Tralala (Cra. 7 No. 6-45, cell tel. 314/850-5543, www.

hostaltralalasalento.com, COP$18,000 dorm, COP$45,000 d). It's hard to miss this in-town option: It's a two-story white house with bright orange wooden trim. At Tralala there are only seven rooms, including a dormitory that sleeps six, making for a chilled-out environment for the guests. Run by a Dutchman, the hostel is spic and span and tastefully decorated. Its minimalist style provides a nice vacation for the eyes. Staff are friendly and knowledgeable, and the kitchen area is a pleasant area to hang out and chitchat with others. There's a sun deck and garden area in case relaxation is needed.

Londoner Tim was one of the first to help transform Salento from a sleepy Paisa pueblo into one of Colombia's top tourist destinations. His Plantation House (Alto de Coronel, Cl. 7 No. 1-04, cell tel. 316/285-2603, www.theplantationhousesalento.com, COP$22,000 dorm, COP$55,000 d), with 24 rooms total, remains one of the top places to get to know Salento and the surrounding areas. Catering to international visitors, this hostel has two houses, one of which is over 100 years old. It's quiet and green around the hostel, and, though you'll be bound to meet other travelers like yourself, there is plenty of space to find a little solitude. Plantation House can organize bike excursions, horseback riding, and hikes to the Valle de Cocora. The owners of the Plantation House have their own organic coffee farm, Finca Don Eduardo (Alto de Coronel, Cl. 7 No. 1-04, cell tel. 316/285-2603, COP$15,000 dorm, COP$35,000 d), about 15 minutes outside of town, which has one private room and one dormitory. This coffee plantation is over 80 years old and set amid lush, rolling hills. It is an environmentally friendly hostel: Solar panels enable guests to have a hot shower, and a rainwater collection system provides that water.

Another excellent hostel-type option is La Serrana Eco-farm and Hostel (Km. 1.5 Vía Palestina Finca, cell tel. 316/296-1890, www.laserrana.com.co, COP$22,000 dorm, COP$55,000 d). It's situated on a bluff with lovely views of coffee farms in every direction. The nine rooms, of various types and sizes, are comfortable, and there is

also a women-only dorm room. Camping is also available for COP$12,000. It's a peaceful place where you can enjoy sunrises and sunsets, go for a walk into town, or just hang out. La Serrana is best known for its delicious (and nutritious) family-style dinners and other meals. Vegetarians always have options, and the cooks make an effort to buy local, fresh food. La Serrana has another, smaller, lodging option, Las Camelias (Km. 1.5 Vía Palestina Finca, cell tel. 316/296-1890, www.laserrana.com.co, COP$70,000 d), a colonial-style house you can see from the hostel. This is geared for couples who want a little more privacy—there are only three rooms. Rooms, drenched with natural light, are spacious, with hardwood floors and fireplaces. Common space is ample with large windows, and there is a kitchen for guest use. From La Serrana it is a short distance to the Finca Ocasa coffee farm.

Centrally located Hostal Ciudad de Segorbe (Cl. 5 No. 4-06, tel. 6/759-3794, www.hostalciudaddesegorbe.com, COP$85,000 d) is a bed and breakfast run by a Colombian and Spanish pair. The renovated house is over 100 years old and is built in the traditional Paisa style. The hostel's eight rooms have high wooden ceilings with gorgeous original geometric designs and small balconies. One room is equipped for guests with disabilities. Pictures of Spanish towns like Segorbe, the hometown of one of the owners, decorate the walls. Excellent service is provided to guests, such as transportation assistance and help with organizing sightseeing activities. There are plans to add more rooms to the hotel in the adjacent lot, which may make it less of an intimate stay, but it's still a good bet.

CAMPING

Four kilometers outside of Salento, on the banks of the Río Quindío, is Camping Monteroca (Valle del Río Quindío, cell tel. 315/413-6862, www.campingmonteroca.com, COP$70,000 cabin, COP$15,000 tent), a sprawling campground catering mostly to Colombian weekenders. The camp has 11 cabins, one of which is called the Hippie

Hilton, and several of them have awesome waterbeds. There is a lot of space for tents here, as well. Monteroca has a restaurant and two bars. Recreational activities such as horseback riding (COP$12,000 per hour), a three-hour hike to nearby waterfalls (COP$25,000), and yoga classes are on offer as well. To get there from Salento, take a Jeep bound for Las Veredas. They leave every 15 minutes from the Plaza Principal during weekends.

Food

Salento offers varied restaurant options, not just the standard *comida típica* fare.

Mojitería (Cl. 4 No. 5-54, cell tel. 310/409-2331, 2pm-11pm daily, COP$18,000) is a lively spot where you can grab a quick bite (appetizers, salads, soups, and pastas) or try one or two of the many mojitos on offer. At night it takes on a bar atmosphere.

It's a real treat to discover a restaurant like **La Eliana** (Cra. 2 No. 6-45, cell tel. 314/660-5987, 10am-9pm daily, COP$20,000), where great service, a cozy atmosphere, and fantastic food are the norm. This Spanish-run spot a few blocks from the center of town is the only place in this part of the woods where you can find curry dishes and gourmet pizzas on the menu. And try as they might, the friendly cocker spaniels aren't allowed to mingle with diners.

One of the best regional food restaurants is **Camino Real Parrilla Bar** (Cra. 6A No. 1-35, cell tel. 314/864-2587, 10am-midnight Sun.-Thurs., 10am-2am Fri.-Sat., COP$18,000). After a grueling climb to the Mirador, this popular place at the top of Calle Real makes for a great stop. The restaurant has outdoor seating and a huge, fairly varied menu with grilled meats, a few salads, and lots of *trucha* (trout). At night it's an *aguardiente,* a popular local drinking hangout.

Alegra (Cra. 6 No. 2-52, cell tel. 301/462-4458, 2pm-8:20pm Mon., Tues., Thurs., and Fri., 12:30pm-8:20pm Sat.-Sun., COP$18,000) is a cute place about a block from the ruckus of Calle Real. Here you can enjoy cilantro pesto pasta, a veggie burger, and a glass of wine as you listen to jazz in the background. It's run by a friendly woman from Bogotá.

Brunch (Cl. 6 No. 3-25, cell tel. 311/757-8082, 6:30am-9:30pm daily, COP$15,000), a hip little joint with graffiti and messages from hundreds of visitors from around the globe decorating the walls, is another restaurant with the international traveler in mind. They do serve brunch, but also breakfast, lunch, and dinner. The menu seems aimed squarely at Americans: Buffalo wings, Philly cheese steak sandwiches, black bean burgers, and peanut butter brownies. Menu items are assigned whimsical names like Wax Palm Pancakes. **Beta Town** (Cl. 7 No. 3-45, cell tel. 321/218-7043, 6pm-midnight daily) is a popular place for burgers, beer, and hanging out. They've even got a *tejo* field, where you can try your luck at this only-in-Colombia sport.

Information and Services

Hostels usually provide the best tourist information, but there is a city-run tourist kiosk, the **Punto de Información Turística** (10am-5pm Wed.-Mon.), in front of the Alcaldía (city offices) in the Plaza Principal.

Getting There and Around

There is frequent bus service from Pereira, Armenia, and other cities to Salento. The last bus from Armenia leaves at 8pm (under COP$4,000). From Pereira, there are four direct buses each weekday, costing under COP$6,000. There is more frequent service on weekends. As Salento is well established on the tourist route, thieves are known to prey on foreigners on late-evening buses traveling from Pereira to Salento. Keep a vigilant eye on your possessions.

Buses to Armenia (every 20 mins., COP$4,000) and Pereira (COP$6,000) depart from the the intersection of Carrera 2 at Calle 5, with the last bus departure at 6pm daily. For Filandia you have to first go to Armenia.

the picturesque Valle de Cocora and its famous wax palms

© ANDREW DIER

🌙 VALLE DE COCORA

The main attraction for most visitors to Salento is seeing the *palmas de cera* (wax palms) that shoot up towards the sky in the Valle de Cocora. These are some of the tallest palms in the world, reaching 50-60 meters high (200 feet), and they can live over 100 years. They have beautiful, smooth, cylindrical trunks with dark rings. In 1985, they were declared to be the national tree of Colombia.

The Valle de Cocora is a 15-kilometer (9-mile) section of the lower Río Quindío valley. Much of it has been turned into pastureland, but, thankfully, the palms have been preserved. The palms look particularly stunning in the denuded pastureland.

The gateway to the valley is the Vereda de Cocora, a stretch of restaurants specializing in trout. This *vereda* (settlement) is a major domestic tourist destination and can get incredibly crowded during holidays and weekends. Most Colombian tourists come for a late lunch and take a stroll along the main road behind the *vereda* to view the palms. However, there are two much

more rewarding excursions: a leisurely 90-minute walk to La Montaña, a ranger station for the local environmental agency, or a more intense five-hour loop through the valley and up the Río Quindío and back via La Montaña.

For the La Montaña hike, continue down the main road beyond the Vereda de Cocoa and pass through the gate of a private farm on the right where a signpost reads "FCA. EL BOSQUE 7.6 KM." Follow a path that meanders six kilometers (four miles) up hills converted to pastureland and then along a ridge on one side of the Valle de Cocora to the ranger station. The views from the path onto the wax palms in the valley and mountainside are stunning. If you opt for the longer hike, that same spectacular scenery comes at the end of a walk that saves the valley of the palms for last, like a delicious dessert.

For the longer hike, take a right through a gate painted blue after the last building in the Vereda de Cocora. After walking about four kilometers (2.5 miles) through pasture, you'll enter the dense forest. The path crisscrosses the trickling Río Quindío. After three kilometers (two miles) you reach the Reserva Acaime (cell tel. 321/636-2818 or 320/788-1981, COP$4,000), a private reserve created to preserve the surrounding cloud forest. With the entrance fee, you can enjoy a complimentary cup of hot chocolate, *agua de panela* (a hot sugary drink), or coffee and watch throngs of hummingbirds of several varieties fly up to feeders. It's quite a show. You can also stay at Acaime, either in private rooms or a large dormitory (COP$40,000 pp including all meals).

From Reserva Acaime, you backtrack a kilometer and then climb a steep path to La Montaña. The last leg of the hike, back from La Montaña to Vereda del Cocora, provides the best and most memorable photo opportunities of the valley and hundreds upon hundreds of wax palms. Make sure your camera batteries are charged, as you'll want to take many pictures. The entire loop takes 4-5 hours. You may want to wear rubber or waterproof boots, as the path along the Río Quindío is muddy. There is no need for a guide.

To get to Vereda del Cocora from Salento, take a Jeep Willy (COP$3,500), which leave the Plaza Pincipal at 6am, 7:30am, 9:30am, and 11:30am each day.

Trek to Finca La Primavera

If you would like to do a longer expedition, you can extend the Valle de Cocora hike beyond Reserva Acaime to the Páramo de Romerales on the border of the Parque Nacional Natural Los Nevados and to Finca La Primavera, a working farm located at an altitude of 3,680 meters (12,075 feet). This excursion allows you to enjoy the transition from cloud forest to *páramo* (highland moor) but requires two days. The path from Acaime continues to Estrella de Agua, a research station, through the Páramo de Romerales and finally Finca Primavera, where you can bunk for COP$10,000 per person and arrange for meals. The entire hike from Vereda de Cocora to Primavera is 13.5 kilometers (8.5 miles) and takes 7-8 hours. This trek does not require camping gear; all you

need is food for snacking. However, it is quite cold at Finca La Primavera, and a sleeping bag makes a difference. Hiring a guide is a good idea as the trail is poorly marked.

From Finca La Primavera, you can continue into the Parque Nacional Natural Los Nevados, hiking to the Nevado del Tolima (5,215 meters/17,110 feet) or the less traveled Paramillo del Quindío (4,750 meters/15,585 feet).

Recommended guides are Páramo Trek (cell tel. 311/745-3761, paramotrek@gmail.com) in Salento and Truman David Alfonso Bejarano (cell tel. 315/292-7395, trumandavid01@gmail. com) in Ibagué, who can organize excursions from Salento or Ibagué.

FILANDIA

To visit an authentic coffee town without the tourists, head to Filandia (pop. 12,000), a cute pueblo between Armenia and Pereira. Sights are few; this town is about atmosphere. The name Filandia has nothing to do with the Nordic country of Finland (which in Spanish is Finlandia).

The focal point on the Parque Central (between Cras. 4-5 and Clls. 6-7) is the church, the Templo María Inmaculada (Cra. 7), which was built in the early 20th century. From the plaza explore the charming streets of the town, including the Calle del Tiempo Detenido (Cl. 7 between Cras. 5-6) and the Calle del Empedrado, two streets of two-story houses made of *bahareque* (a natural material) adorned by colorful doors and windows. Stop by the town's oldest construction, the Droguería Bristol (Cra. 6 No. 5-63) along the way. A nice view of the countryside can be had near the *clínica mental* (mental hospital; Cra. 8 No. 7-55). On the street pick up one of Filandia's famous reed baskets.

On the road towards Quimbaya, just outside of town, is the wooden Ecoparque Mirador de las Colinas Iluminadas (10am-7pm Mon.-Fri., 10am-9pm Sat.-Sun., COP$3,000), which looks like a wooden spaceship. From the top are nice views of the countryside, and inside, looking down, is a strange mosaic of a giant blue butterfly. On the way towards the *mirador*, pop into one of the many handicraft shops, where you can browse baskets until the cows come home.

Accommodations and Food

Accommodations and restaurants in Filandia are limited. In a traditional Paisa house, the Hostal La Posada del Compadre (Cra. 6 No. 8-06, tel. 6/758-3054, cell tel. 313/335-9771, www.laposadadelcompadre.com, COP$60,000 d) offers a handful of rooms and ample outdoor hangout space. Rooms are large, beds are adequate, breakfast is included, and the prices are reasonable.

With a prime location on the main square, the Hostal Tibouchina (Cl. 6A No. 5-05, tel. 6/758-2646, COP$40,000 pp d) has seven rooms and pleasant common areas, including a large kitchen. It's on the second floor above a café/bar. The interior rooms, which lack windows, are on the stuffy side. On the other hand, if you get one of the rooms facing the street, you may hear music and the goings-on in the plaza until the wee hours on weekends.

The 🌒 Hostal Colina de Lluvia (Cra. 4 No. 5-15, COP$25,000 dorm, COP$60,000 d private) opened in mid-2013 and is easily the best place to stay in Filandia. Tastefully decorated rooms are spic and span with comfortable beds, and there is a small garden patio.

Candlelit tables, lounge music, and art on the walls—you won't believe your eyes when you see 🌒 Helena Adentro (Cra. 7 No. 8-01, cell tel. 312/873-9825, noon-2am weekends). Started by a New Zealander and a Paisa, it's by far the coolest spot in Filandia, Quindío, and perhaps this side of Medellín. Cured meats and goat cheeses come from local farmers, along with the coffee. They have their own brand of coffee but also serve coffee from other regions of Colombia, using different brewing techniques. Locals keep coming back for the inventive libations here, such as the house cocktail, the Adentro Helena (aguardiente, *lulo* juice, and lime).

The popular place for a cappuccino is Jahn Café (Cl. 6 No. 5-45, 7:30am-midnight Mon.-Fri., 7:30am-2am Sat.-Sun.).

Information and Services

The Filandia tourist office is in the Casa del Artesano (Cra. 5 at Cl. 7, 2nd floor, tel. 6/758-2172, 7am-noon and 1:30pm-4:30pm Mon.-Fri.).

Getting There and Around

Buses to Filandia leave from Armenia (COP$4,000, every 20 minutes) and Pereira (COP$5,000, hourly) all day long until around 8pm. These circulate the town picking up passengers, especially on Carrera 7.

PEREIRA AND VICINITY

In Pereira (pop. 465,000), the capital of the Risaralda department, you can get your boots muddy, see exotic birds, and experience the tropical Andean forest during the day, then later enjoy a good meal out or hit the town until late. Pereira is perfectly situated for day trips to the countryside, be it elegant haciendas or natural parks such as Santuario de Flora y Fauna Otún-Quimbaya. In town, you can easily see the major sights of interest in one day: the spectacular cathedral, the Plaza de Bolívar with its statue of a nude Simón Bolívar on horseback charging ahead, and the Museo de Arte de Pereira. Manizales, Armenia, and Salento are within one hour driving or riding of Pereira.

Sights

Downtown, in the Plaza de Bolívar (Clls. 19-20 and Cras. 7-8) stands a bronze sculpture by Rodrigo Arenas Betancourt depicting the Liberator Simón Bolívar on horseback charging ahead to fight the Spaniards—naked. Facing the plaza is the Nuestra Señora de la Pobreza Catedral (Cl. 20 No. 7-30, tel. 6/335-6545, masses every hour 6am-noon and 5pm Mon.-Sat., 6am-noon and 5pm-8pm Sun.). The cathedral was originally built in 1890, using industrial-era building techniques, and was damaged by an earthquake, needing to be almost completely reconstructed. It was rebuilt with a wooden

ceiling and supports made from cumin laurel, a tree native to Colombia that is now endangered.

The Museo de Arte de Pereira (Av. Las Américas No. 19-88, tel. 6/317-2828, www.museo-deartedepereira.com, 9am-noon and 2pm-6pm Tues.-Fri., 10am-5pm Sat.-Sun., free) is one of the best art museums in the region, and deserving of a visit. It features temporary exhibitions of contemporary Latin American artists. It's south of downtown.

In the Parque Olaya Herrera (between Cras. 13-14 and Clls. 19-23) is the well-preserved Antigua Estación del Tren, a photogenic old train station. There is a Megabus station in the park, and the park is a nice place for a morning jog.

The Zoológico Matecaña (Av. 30 de Agosto, tel. 6/314-2636, www.zoopereira.org, 9am-6pm daily, COP$15,000), located within screeching, howling, and roaring distance of the airport, has an extensive section on Colombian animals. It's better than many zoos in Colombia; however, big cats, including Colombian jaguars, have little space to move about.

The Viaducto César Gavíria Trujillo is a modern cable bridge that connects Pereira with its industrial neighbor of Dosquebradas. It's a point of reference and source of city pride. It is named for former president César Gavíria, who is from Pereira and who served as president during the early 1990s.

Recreation

For bike tours and rentals, contact Retro Ciclas (cell tel. 310/540-7327 or 312/437-4882, www.mt-btourscolombia.com). One of the more popular tours is a trip to the village of Estación Pereira (COP$86,000), where in the town you'll take two different and exciting means of transportation: a *brujita,* a motorcycle-powered cart that zooms along old train tracks, and later a *garrucha,* which is a gondola-like metallic basket that transports passengers over the Río Cauca. Another trip on offer is along the Río Otún (COP$80,000) to the Santuario de Flora y Fauna Otún-Quimbaya.

Accommodations

In town, it's best to stay in the Circunvalar area. The Centro has options, but prices are comparable to hotels on the Circunvalar, where you can walk without much concern at night and there are plenty of restaurants and nightlife spots nearby.

The C Kolibrí Hostel (Cl. No. 16-35, tel. 6/331-3955, cell tel. 321/646-9275, www.kolibri-hostel.com, COP$22,000 dorm, COP$60,000 d) is a welcome newcomer to Pereira, filling a void of budget accommodations for international clientele near the Circunvalar. In addition to a mix of private rooms and dorms, Kolibrí has two long-stay apartments. It's run by a Dutch-Colombian couple who have traveled extensively in the area to some off-the-map places, and they offer tours, such as to the village of Estación Pereira, to the Santuario de Flora y Fauna Otún-Quimbaya, and an interesting orchid tour. Bars, restaurants, and malls are within walking distance from the hostel. Great breakfasts are offered on the deck, where they also have a barbecue grill.

The Hotel Movich (Cra. 13 No. 15-73, tel. 6/311-3300, COP$249,000 d) is a good option if you like comfort, don't want any surprises, and want the conveniences that the Circunvalar offers. It's across the street from the Iglesia de Carmen. The pool (usually open until 9pm) and gym (open 24 hours) are quite nice. A massive breakfast buffet is included in the room rate.

A restful sleep is assured at the Hotel Don Alfonso (Cra. 13 No. 12-37, tel. 6/333-0909, www.donalfonsohotel.com, COP$240,000 d), a small boutique-style hotel on the main nightlife and shopping drag of the Avenida Circunvalar. It has 11 comfortable air-conditioned rooms, each with inviting beds covered by quilts.

HACIENDAS

Within minutes of the Pereira's bright lights are some gorgeous and luxurious hacienda hotels. Some of them are popular places for special events, such as weddings on the weekend and corporate seminars during the week.

Hacienda Malabar (Km. 7 Vía a Cerritos, Entrada 6, tel. 6/337-9206, www.hotelmalabar.com, COP$257,500 d) is an authentic hacienda with seven rooms, ample gardens to wander, and a pool. The wooden ceilings with their geometric designs and tile floors with Spanish Mudejar designs throughout the house are spectacular.

C Villa Martha (Km. 9 Vía a Marsella, 1 km from the main road, tel. 6/322-9994, cell tel. 310/421-5920, www.fincavillamartha.com, COP$75,000 pp with meals) offers the most affordable coffee farm experience. Here you can kick back and relax, take a dip in a pool that has "Villa Martha" written on the bottom, stroll the countryside, and take a tour of the coffee plantation. It's not luxurious, but the warm hospitality of the *finca* (farm) owners, Martha and her husband, Rafael, more than compensates. Rooms by the pool are nicer. Villa Martha doesn't allow non-guests to visit for the day.

C Castilla Casa de Huespedes (Km. 10 Vía a Cerritos, tel. 6/337-9045, cell tel. 315/499-9545, www.haciendacastilla.com, COP$281,000 d), built in the 19th century, is set amid fruit trees and has a pool to boot. The nine rooms are lovely, and staff are friendly. Once there, at this serene spot in the countryside, you'll probably not even be aware of the fact that a fried chicken restaurant is just around the corner along the highway! They make their own jam here, and a majestic cedar tree near the pool area looks even more regal when illuminated at night.

The Hacienda San José (Km. 4 Vía Pereira-Cerritos, Entrada 16, Cadena El Tigre, tel. 6/313-2612, www.haciendahotelsanjose.com, COP$275,000-310,000 d) was built in 1888 and has been in the Jaramillo family for generations. It's in the countryside, and the entrance to it, lined with palms, is a dramatic one. The home is spectacular, and the lovely wooden floors make a satisfying creak when you step on the planks. Service is impeccable and the restaurant, excellent. The grounds make for a nice late afternoon stroll, and you can admire an enormous and regal old *samán* tree, well into its second century of life, as you dine alfresco. Living Trips (www.livingtrips.com) manages this hotel, and they can arrange day trip excursions for you. The restaurant is open to the public, and members of the public can also come for the day and enjoy the pool. It is almost always booked on weekends and during holidays. This gorgeous hacienda is a particularly popular place for weddings on weekends. The Matecaña airport is only 10 minutes away.

Luxury hotel Sazagua (Km. 7 Vía Cerritos, Entrada 4, tel. 6/337-9895, www.sazagua.com, COP$446,000 d) is not technically a hacienda, as it is located in a country club type environment. Here attention to detail reigns. The 10 rooms are impeccable, the common space is inviting, the gardens are perfectly manicured (surrounded by elegant heliconia flowers, birds, and the occasional iguana), and you can lounge by the pool or enjoy a massage at the spa. Nonguests can enjoy the spa facilities for a separate charge. It's not a traditional hacienda, but it sure feels good there.

Food

Pereira makes it easy for visitors, gastronomically speaking. All the top restaurants are in more or less the same area, along and nearby the Avenida Circunvalar.

Mama Flor (Cl. 11 No. 15-12, tel. 6/335-4713, noon-10pm Mon.-Sat., noon-5pm Sun., COP$15,000) is a cute joint catering to meat-lovers with mostly open-air seating and old photographs of Pereira decorating the walls. It's mostly a lunch

place. Grilled beef options like tri-tip (in Colombia called *punta de anca*) are menu favorites.

The specialty at somewhat swanky Mediterraneo (Av. Circunvalar No. 4-47, tel. 6/331-0397, noon-2am Mon.-Thurs., noon-3am Sat., noon-1am Sun., COP$25,000) is seafood, but the menu is varied. The lighting is a little on the dark side, but the restaurant is all open-air.

Ambar Diego Panesso (Cra. 17 No. 9-50, tel. 6/344-7444, noon-3pm and 6pm-10pm Mon.-Sat., COP$30,000) serves up elaborate dishes like portobello mushrooms stuffed with apple puree and bacon bits to the Pereira elite. While vegetarian dishes are mostly nonexistent on the menu, the kitchen will gladly take on the challenge and whip up a pasta dish for you. It's in the upscale Pinares neighborhood. Another restaurant on the elegant side is El Mirador (Av. Circunvalar at Cl. 4, Colina, tel. 6/331-2141, noon-2am Mon.-Sat., COP$30,000), a steakhouse that has an incredible view of the city. There's an extensive list of Argentinian wines.

The menu at El Meson Español (Cl. 14 No. 25-57, tel. 6/321-5636, noon-3pm and 7pm-midnight daily, COP$22,000) runs the gamut from paellas (the house specialty) to pad Thai.

Dine under a giant Italian flag at the open-air Portobello (Cra. 15 No. 11-55, tel. 6/325-0802, noon-3pm and 6pm-10pm Mon.-Wed., noon-3pm and 6pm-11pm Thurs.-Sat., noon-9pm Sun., COP$25,000), the top address for pasta and other Italian favorites, where pizzas are cooked in a wood-burning oven.

Diego Parrilla (Cl. 10B No. 15-09, tel. 6/333-8503, cell tel. 317/402-1980, noon-11pm Mon.-Sat daily, COP$30,000) is a popular steakhouse. It's in the pleasant Los Alpes area, not far from the Circunvalar.

For a hearty Colombian meal, like a big bowl of *ajiaco* (a filling potato-based stew), or to hang out and have a couple of beers at night, La Ruana (Av. Circunvalar No. 12-08, tel. 6/325-0115, 8am-2am Mon.-Sat., 8am-10pm Sun., COP$20,000) is the place to go on the Avenida Circunvalar.

Bermeo (tel. 6/333-0909, noon-3pm and 6pm-11pm daily, COP$25,000), which specializes in international cuisine, adjoins Hotel Don Alfonso. While they don't have much in the way of veggie options, they can accommodate vegetarians.

Two always reliable and reasonably priced Colombian chain restaurants that have healthy options on their menus hold prime space in the Centro Comercial Parque Arboleda (Circunvalar No. 5-20, www.parquearboleda. com). Archie's (tel. 6/317-0600, www.archiespizza.com, 8am-11pm daily, COP$22,000) has great pizzas (try the thin-crust *pizzas rústicas*) and salads. Its location on the top floor, with a breezy terrace, is a cool one. They also deliver. Directly below on the ground floor, meals at Crepes & Waffles (tel. 6/331-5189, www.crepesywaffles.com.co, noon-9pm Sun.-Wed., noon-10pm Thurs.-Sat., COP$25,000) serves both savory and sweet crêpes, including many vegetarian options. Desserts, such as mini-waffles with chocolate sauce and vanilla ice cream, are hard to resist.

Information and Services

In Pereira, you can call 123 for any type of emergency.

There is a small tourist information booth in the lobby of the Centro Cultural Lucy Tejada (Cl. 10 No. 16-60, tel. 6/311-6544, www.pereiraculturayturismo.gov.co, 8am-noon and 2pm-6:30pm Mon.-Fri.).

Getting There and Around

Excellent bus connections are available between Pereira and most major cities. The Terminal de Transportes de Pereira (Cl. 17 No. 23-157, tel. 6/315-2323, www.terminaldepereira.com) is relatively close to the Avenida Circunvalar area. It is clean.

The articulated bus rapid transit system, the Megabus (tel. 6/335-1010), has three routes and connects with 28 intra-city buses. It's not terribly convenient for those staying near the Avenida Circunvalar, unfortunately.

The Aeropuerto Matecaña (Av. 30 de Agosto, tel. 6/314-2765) is pint-sized, and about a 10-minute ride east from the city. It's quite convenient for those planning on staying at one of the several haciendas in that area. The two largest Colombian airliners, Avianca (Av. Circunvalar No. 8B-23, tel. 6/333-0990, www.avianca.com, 8am-1pm and 2:30pm-6pm Mon.-Fri., 8am-noon Sat.) and LAN (Cl. 19 No. 8-34, Local 102, 8am-6pm Mon.-Fri., 9am-1pm Sat.) serve Pereira. Panamanian-based Copa (Av. Circunvalar No. 8B-51, Edificio Bancafe, Local 103, Col. toll-free tel. 01/800-011-2600, www.copaair.com, 8am-6pm Mon.-Fri., 9am-noon Sat.) has nonstop flights to Panama City five days a week. Budget Viva Colombia (www.vivacolombia.co) flies nonstop between Pereira and the Caribbean cities of Cartagena (4 weekly flights) and Santa Marta (3 weekly flights).

For those looking to rent a car, Hertz (airport tel. 6/314-2678, www.hertz.com, 8am-6pm Mon.-Fri., 8am-noon Sat.) has an office at the airport.

VALLE DEL RÍO OTÚN

A visit to the Valle del Río Otún (Río Otún Valley) between Pereira and the Laguna del Otún is an interesting, highly enjoyable, and easy to organize introduction to Andean cloud forests. There are many possibilities for visiting the valley, from day trips out of Pereira to multi-day excursions, with very pleasant lodging facilities in the Santuario de Flora y Fauna Otún-Quimbaya and Parque Regional Natural Ucumarí.

The Río Otún flows 78 kilometers (48 miles) from the Laguna del Otún to the Río Cauca and is the main source of water for Pereira. The conservation of the upper segment of the river, from Pereira to the Laguna del Otún, has been a success story, thanks to reforestation land protection efforts.

PLANNING YOUR TIME

The Santuario de Flora y Fauna Otún-Quimbaya is 14.4 kilometers (9 miles) southeast of Pereira along the Río Otún. The Parque Regional Natural Ucumarí is 6.6 kilometers (4 miles) upriver.

You can do day trips out of Pereira to either, but

the Río Otún

don't try to do both in one day. Santuario de Flora y Fauna Otún-Quimbaya is easily accessible by public transportation, and the main nature trails can be visited in one day. However, getting to Parque Regional Natural Ucumarí involves public transportation and a two-hour hike. It can be visited on a long day trip but it is much preferable to spend a night or two at the comfortable Pastora visitor center in the midst of the Andean forest. You can combine a visit to both, visiting Santuario de Flora y Fauna Otún-Quimbaya and then spending a day or two in Parque Regional Natural Ucumarí.

December and July-August are drier months, and considered the best time for a hike to the Laguna del Otún. However, during mid-December through mid-January and Semana Santa (Holy Week) in March or April the trails can be packed with hikers, as this is high season for Colombians. The hike through Parque Regional Natural Ucumarí to the Laguna del Otún is very popular then, and there can be over a hundred hikers camping each night at that mountain lake.

Santuario de Fauna y Flora Otún-Quimbaya

The **Santuario de Fauna y Flora Otún-Quimbaya** (Km. 4.5 Vía Florida-El Cedral, Vereda La Suiza, cell tel. 313/695-4305, www.parquesnacionales.gov.co, COP$5,000) covers 489 hectares (1,208 acres) of highly biodiverse Andean tropical forest at altitudes between 1,750 and 2,250 meters (5,740 and 7,380 feet). The vegetation is exuberant, and there are animal-viewing opportunities. The park is home to more than 200 species of birds, including endangered multicolored tanagers and the large *pava caucana* (Cauca guan). And, although you may not see them, you'll definitely hear the *mono aulladores* (howler monkeys). They make quite a brouhaha.

The main activities at the park are guided walks along three nature paths led by knowledgeable and enthusiastic guides from a local community ecotourism organization, the **Asociación Comunitaria Yarumo Blanco** (cell tel. 312/200-7711, yarumoblanco2009@hotmail.com). The tours cost COP$35,000 for one path, COP$70,000 for two, and COP$80,000 for all three (per group of any size). Visitors can also rent mountain bikes (COP$10,000 all day) and ride along the main road bordering the crystalline Río Otún.

The visitors center, also run by the association, offers simple but comfortable lodging (COP$32,000-42,000 pp) and meals (COP$6,000-9,000).

To get to Otún-Quimbaya from Pereira, take a bus operated by **Transportes Florida** (tel. 6/331-0488, COP$4,000, 90 mins.) from Calle 12 and Carrera 9 in Pereira. On weekdays, the bus departs at 7am, 9am, and 3pm. On weekends there is an additional bus at noon. The buses return from Otún-Quimbaya at approximately 9:30am, 11:30am, and 5:30pm.

Parque Regional Natural Ucumarí

The **Parque Regional Natural Ucumarí** is 6.6 kilometers (4 miles) southwest of Santuario Flora y Fauna Otún-Quimbaya. This regional park covers an area of 3,986 hectares (9,850 acres) of Andean tropical forest at altitudes between 1,800 and 2,600 meters (5,900 and 8,500 feet). The main path follows the Río Otún through lush cloud forests, with waterfalls feeding into the river. The park is a wonderful place to view nature, with more than 185 species of birds.

The starting point of the main path is El Cedral, a small *vereda* (settlement) southwest of Santuario Flora y Fauna Otún-Quimbaya. The path is a well-trod one (by humans and horses) and is often muddy and rocky. It is best to take rubber or waterproof boots. It takes about 2.5 hours to climb to the main La Pastora visitors center, six kilometers from El Cedral.

If you are on a day trip from Pereira, you can have lunch at the visitors center (COP$9,000 pp) and set off on one of three nature hikes before returning to El Cedral to catch the last bus at 5pm. Even better, you can spend a night or two in the clean and very cozy dormitory-style rooms (COP$22,000 pp). As the temperature begins to drop in the late afternoon, you can sit by the lodge's fireplace and sip hot chocolate and eat cheese (as is the custom in Colombia). There is no electricity, making a stay at La Pastora truly restful. To make a reservation, contact the ecotourism organization Fecomar (cell tel. 312/200-7711, fecomar.anp@hotmail.com, www.fecomar.com.co). They can arrange horses, if you would rather ride than hike up.

Past La Pastora, the path continues 13 kilometers to the Laguna del Otún in the Parque Nacional Natural Los Nevados.

To get to El Cedral take the Transportes Florida bus (tel. 6/331-0488, COP$5,000, 2 hrs.) from Calle 12 and Carrera 9 in Pereira. On weekdays, the bus departs at 7am, 9am, and 3pm. On weekends there is an additional bus at noon. The buses return from Santuario Flora y Fauna Otún-Quimbaya at approximately 9am, 11am, and 5pm.

SANTA ROSA DE CABAL

The dusty town of Santa Rosa de Cabal means one thing to most Colombians: *termales* (hot springs). To get to the most well-known springs you'll have to pass through Santa Rosa de Cabal. In town, at the Parque las Araucarias (between Cras. 14-15 and Clls. 12-13), the main square, there are juices to be drank, *chorizo santarosano* sausages to be eaten (a specialty here), handicrafts to be bought, and people to be watched. The other point of interest is the Santuario La Milagrosa (Cl. 7 at Cra. 14, tel. 6/368-5201 or 6/368-5168), a generally drab modern church with a fantastic stained glass window.

Hot Springs

There are two *termales* (hot springs) near Santa Rosa de Cabal: Termales de Santa Rosa de Cabal (Km. 9 Vía Termales, tel. 6/364-5500, www.termales.com.co, 9am-11:30pm daily, COP$14,000-31,000) and Termales San Vicente (18 km east of Santa Rosa de Cabal, tel. 6/333-3433, www.sanvicente.com.co, 8am-midnight daily, COP$19,000-60,000). Both are wildly popular with Colombian families on weekends and holidays, and are quieter during the week. Both springs offer transportation from Pereira, and entry fees drop during the week.

Built in 1945, the Termales de Santa Rosa de Cabal hot springs are closer to Santa Rosa de Cabal. There are two areas in the complex. The first area, on the left as you enter the park, was recently built and is called the Termales Balneario. These consist of three large pools for adults and one for children. This area is the most popular for day-trip visitors.

The oldest part of the complex, called Termales de Hotel (hours vary Mon.-Fri., COP$24,000), is farther on at the base of some spectacular waterfalls of cool and pure mountain waters. The highest waterfall drops some 175 meters (575 feet). If you choose to stay the night, there are three options. La Cabaña (COP$183,000 pp, meals incl.) is the newest and most comfortable place to stay and has 17 rooms. La Cabaña guests are allowed entry to the Termales Balneario, the Termales de Hotel, and their own small private pool. The advantage of staying at one of the hotels is that you can enjoy full use of the pools from 6am on, before the day-trip crowd begins arriving at 9am.

At both Termales Balneario and Termales de Hotel, there are additional activities on offer, such as a guided nature walk (COP$14,000) to some waterfalls—wear shoes with traction for this, the path is slippery—and spa treatments such as massages (COP$60,000, 45 mins.) and other services in a shabby-looking spa area.

The San Vicente hot springs are more remote, but the scenery of rolling hills, mountains in the distance, and farms is enchanting. Particularly scenic are the *pozos de amor,* small natural pools the size of whirlpools that perfectly fit two. The all-inclusive *pasadia* (day pass) option with transportation costs COP$60,000. Buses leave Pereira at 8am, returning at 5pm. San Vicente also offers accommodations, with cabins and a small hotel. A cabin for two people costs COP$173,000 per person without meals.

Accommodations and Food

The bucolic countryside outside of Santa Rosa is home to many roadside, family-style restaurants. The best two are run by the same owner. On the road towards the Termales de Santa Rosa, Mamatina (Km. 1 Vía Termales, La Leona, tel. 6/363-4899, 9am-10pm daily, COP$18,000) specializes in trout covered with sausage, *sancocho* (a meaty stew), and grilled meats. They can also accommodate vegetarians, usually a nutritious meal of beans and rice. Next door to the restaurant is their hotel by the same name (tel. 6/363-4899), which offers clean and comfortable rooms ranging in price from COP$40,000 per person to COP$140,000 for the suite with a hot tub. Horseback riding and walks through the countryside can be arranged here.

On the way towards Termales de San Vicente is their other, newer hotel. The (Hospedaje Don Lolo (Km. 5 Vía Termales San Vicente, cell tel. 316/698-6797, hospedajedonlol@gmail.com, COP$50,000 pp d) is a hotel on a farm with cows, pigs, fish, horses, and dogs. If you're interested, you can lend a hand milking a cow or two. Some walks through the countryside are options as well, such as to an old Indian cemetery, to a big waterfall, and

sunny street in Belalcázar

© ANDREW DIER

through jungle to see birds and butterflies. The countryside views and fresh air are delightful. If you're lucky, you may be able to see the Nevado del Ruiz in the distance in the early morning. The Don Lolo (Km. 5 Vía Termales San Vicente, cell tel. 316/698-6797) restaurant just down the road has a lot of personality and is a popular stopping off point going to or returning from the Termales de San Vicente.

BELALCÁZAR

The coffee and plantain town of Belalcázar rests impossibly on a ridge, with fantastic views of the Valle de Cauca on one side and the Valle del Río Risaralda on the other. Besides the incredible views, Belalcázar, an agricultural town off the tourist map, offers the visitor pure coffee region authenticity. Belalcázar has a distinct architecture, with its houses covered with colorful zinc sheets to protect against strong winds.

Built in 1954 in hopes of preventing further bloodshed during the bloody Violencia period, the 45.5-meter-high (149-foot-high) Monumento a Cristo Rey (Km. 1 Vía Pereira-Belalcázar, COP$3,000) has become the symbol of this town. To get to the top of the statue of Jesus, you'll have to climb 154 steps. From atop, on a clear day, you can see six Colombian departments: Caldas, Risaralda, Quindío, Valle del Cauca, Tolima, and Chocó; and both Central and Occidental mountain ranges. The other attraction in town is the Eco Parque La Estampilla hike (1.5 km, open daylight hours, free). It's on the northeast side of town, a 10-minute walk from the Parque Bolívar (Clls. 15-16 and Cras. 4-5), in which you can wander a winding path through forests of *guadua* (bamboo).

The best time to check out Belalcázar life at its most vibrant is on market day—Saturday—when farmers from the countryside converge into town to sell coffee beans, plantains, pineapples, and other crops. On this day the Parque Bolívar buzzes with activity as Jeep Willys, packed with farmers and market-goers, come and go all day long. It's quite a carnival atmosphere.

The best hotel in town is the Hotel Balcón Colonial (Cra. 4A No. 12-10, tel. 6/860-2433, COP$35,000 d). It's clean, cool, and basic, having just nine rooms.

Getting There

It is 45 kilometers (29 miles) from Pereira to Belalcázar. Buses leave from the Pereira Terminal de Transportes (Cl. 17 No. 23-157, Pereira, tel. 6/315-2323). Flota Occidental (tel. 6/321-1655) is the bus company that serves Belalcázar (COP$6,000, 1.5 hrs.).

SANTUARIO

It's worth the arduous journey to this remote village on a mountaintop in the Cordillera Occidental (Western Mountains) just to take a photo of its famous Calle Real, dotted with stately Paisa houses that have been done up in a rainbow of colors. Calle Real is one of the most photographed streets in Colombia.

On Saturdays, campesinos come into town to sell their coffee, cacao, sugarcane, and other crops.

There is so much activity on market day in the Plaza de Bolívar (between Clls. 6-7 and Cras. 5-6) that you'll be tempted to find a front row seat in a café and take it all in: produce and coffee being unloaded and loaded, Jeep Willys filled with standing-room-only passengers arriving and departing, farmers drinking beer in taverns, women selling sweets in the park, and children being children. Many farmers, money in hand, whoop it up in town and stay the night.

Although Santuario is indeed picture-perfect, it's far better to continue on to the Parque Nacional Natural Tatamá than to spend the night in Santuario, even if you are not interested in doing any hiking or trekking. Hotels in town are not recommended.

There is regular bus transportation from the Terminal de Transportes de Pereira (Cl. 17 No. 23-157, Pereira, tel. 6/315-2323) to Santuario. Flota Occidental (tel. 6/321-1655) makes this two-hour trip (COP$6,000) three times a day: 6:45am, noon, and 5:20pm.

PARQUE MUNICIPAL NATURAL PLANES DE SAN RAFAEL

Located in the remote, little visited Cordillera Occidental (Western Mountains), the Tatamá Massif contains one of the world's few remaining pristine *páramos* (highland moors). The topography of the mountain range is very broken, especially the jagged Cerro Tatamá (4,250 meters/13,945 feet), which is the highest point in the Cordillera Occidental. The range is highly biodiverse, with an estimated 564 species of orchids and 402 species of birds. It is also home to pumas, jaguars, and *osos anteojos,* the only breed of bear in Colombia. The central part of the massif is protected by the 15,900-hectare (39,300-acre) Parque Natural Nacional Tatamá.

Access to Tatamá is through the Parque Municipal Natural Planes de San Rafael, which acts as a buffer zone on the eastern side of Tatamá near the town of Santuario, but which is an attraction in itself.

The Parque Municipal Natural Planes de San Rafael (10 km from Santuario, cell tel 311/719-1717, http://planesdesanrafael.blogspot.com) covers an area of 11,796 hectares (29,149 acres) of cloud forest between the altitudes of 2,000 and 2,600 meters, with significant patches of primary growth. The main activities are nature walks conducted by friendly and knowledgeable guides of a local community organization, the Asociación de Guías e Interpretes Ambientales (GAIA), many of whom got their start through participation in groups of youth bird-watchers.

Within the park there are four main paths. The shortest, called the Lluvia de Semillas (Rainfall of Seeds), allows visitors to see a forest in recuperation. It is a one-kilometer (0.6-mile) loop through land that was once used for cattle grazing and, over the past 15 years, has been slowly returning to a forest. The 9.6-kilometer (6-mile) round-trip Cascadas trail is a strenuous path to the border of the Parque Nacional Natural Tatamá at an elevation of 2,600 meters. It crisscrosses the Río San Rafael and culminates at a group of waterfalls. Along the way you can see a great variety of birds and large patches of primary forest. The hike takes 3.5 hours up and 2.5 hours down. The 12-kilometer (7.5-mile) Quebrada Risaralda hike takes six hours and can be combined into a loop with the Cascadas hike. Finally, the Laguna Encantada path is a nine-kilometer (5.5-mile) circuit that takes five hours and is especially good for bird-watching, with the possibility of viewing many hummingbirds. The best time for these hikes is early in the morning. Costs for these excursions are COP$25,000-35,000 per group of any size.

Parque Nacional Natural Tatamá

From Parque Municipal Natural Planes de San Rafael it is also possible to organize excursions into the Parque Nacional Natural Tatamá (tel. 6/368-7964, www.parquesnacionales.gov.co), located at the highest point of the Cordillera Occidental between the departments of Chocó, Risaralda, and Valle del Cauca. Though it is not officially open to ecotourism, the folks at GAIA can organize an excursion that requires at least two nights of camping. The first day involves a 12-kilometer (7.5-mile), eight-hour hike to a campground at 3,200 meters. The following day you explore the upper reaches of the Tatamá, with the unusual shrub-covered *páramo* (high tropical mountain ecosystem), craggy outcrops, and deep gorges. From the top you can see the Chocó lowlands. You return by nightfall to camp and return to Parque Municipal Natural Planes de San Rafael on the following day.

Accommodations

The clean, comfortable, and quite cozy lodge (COP$20,000 pp) at the Parque Municipal Natural Planes de San Rafael visitors center accommodates 40 people. Meals (COP$6,000-9,000) are nothing short of delicious. To reserve lodging, contact the ecotourism organization FECOMAR (cell tel. 312/200-7711, fecomar.anp@hotmail.com, www.fecomar.com.co) or call the park administrator (cell tel. 311/719-1717).

Getting There

To get to the Parque Municipal Natural Planes de San Rafael visitors center and lodge, pick up one of the Jeeps that leave from the main square in Santuario each day at 7am and 3pm. A taxi can also take you for COP$20,000.

IBAGUÉ

Ibagué (pop. 593,000) is the capital city of the Tolima department. It is a hot city of traffic jams that does not seduce many travelers. It is, however, a city of music and hosts several music festivals each year. It's hard to believe, but just to the west of Ibagué, a city in one of the most important tropical-fruit-producing regions in Colombia, looms the Nevado del Tolima, a snowcapped volcano in the eastern side of the Parque Nacional Natural Los Nevados. Ibagué is a great launch pad for the challenge of ascending to that mountain.

Sights

Should you have some time to spend in Ibagué, a handful of sights are worth taking a look. Shade is not an issue at the Plaza de Bolívar (between Cras. 2-3 and Clls. 9-10): It's full of huge, centuries-old trees.

Staff at the tourist kiosk in the plaza in front of the Catedral Inmaculada Concepción (Cl. 10 No. 1-129, tel. 8/263-3451, 7am-noon and 2:30pm-7:30pm daily) can suggest hiking excursions and tips on trekking up to the Nevado del Tolima. The Banco de la República (Cra. 3A No. 11-26, tel. 8/263-0721, 8:30am-6pm Mon.-Fri., 8:30am-1pm Sat., free) always has an exhibit in its one exhibition hall on the second floor. It's just off of Calle Peatonal (Cra. 3 between Clls. 10-15), which is refreshingly free from cars and motorbikes.

The Conservatorio del Tolima (Cra. 1 between Clls. 9-10, tel. 8/826-1852, www.conservatoriodeltolima.edu.co, open only for concerts) is perhaps Ibagué's claim to fame and the reason it calls itself the "Capital Musical de Colombia." A few bars from the Colombian national anthem are painted on the exterior of the yellow republican-era building.

Music festivals take place in the city year-round, including the Festival Nacional de la Musica Colombiana (www.fundacionmusicaldecolombia.com, Mar.), the Festival de Jazz (May), and the Festival Folclórico Colombiano (www.festivalfolclorico.com, June or July).

The Museo de Arte del Tolima (Cra. 7 No. 5-93, tel. 8/273-2840, www.museodeartedeltolima.org, 10am-6pm daily, COP$3,000) is a small museum with a permanent collection and temporary exhibition space dedicated to contemporary Colombian artists. A leafy park in this pleasant part of town is the Parque Centenario (Cra. 6 between Clls. 8-10). Along with usual park goings-on, cultural events are often held in an amphitheater.

Accommodations and Food

The Hotel Ambeima (Cra. 3 No. 13-32, tel. 8/263-4300, www.hotelambeima.com, COP$89,000 d) is downtown on the Calle Peatonal and is a decent midrange choice. The best hotel in town is the Hotel Estelar Altamira (Cra. 1A No. 45-50, tel. 8/266-6111, COP$203,000 d). There are no hostels that cater to international backpackers.

The trendy dining and drinking spot in Ibagué is 15 stories high, with a superb bird's-eye view of the city and the Parque Nacional Natural Los Nevados. Altavista (Cra. 2 at Cl. 11, tel. 8/277-1381, noon-midnight Mon.-Wed., noon-3am Thurs.-Sat., noon-4pm Sun., COP$25,000) has a little bit of everything: Asian-inspired dishes, tapas, and even several vegetarian options. The decor and atmosphere are all South Beach. As the sun slips behind the mountains in the distance, bartenders swing into full motion as Altavista turns into a *play* (fashionable) nightclub scene.

Getting There and Around

The Terminal de Transportes (Cra. 2 No. 20-86, tel. 8/261-8122, www.terminalibague.com) is in a rough part of town, so you should take a cab to and from the bus station. For the most part, Ibagué is not a walkable city, except in the center of town. From the Ibagué airport, Aeropuerto Nacional Perales (Vía al Aeropuerto, tel. 8/267-6096), there are nonstop flights to Bogotá and Medellín.

MAP SYMBOLS

▬▬▬	Expressway	【	Highlight	✈	Airport	⚓	Golf Course
▬▬▬	Primary Road	○	City/Town	✈	Airfield	🅿	Parking Area
▬▬▬	Secondary Road	◉	State Capital	▲	Mountain	▲	Archaeological Site
▬▬▬	Unpaved Road	⊛	National Capital	✦	Unique Natural Feature	♦	Church
▬▬▬	Trail	★	Point of Interest			🔲	Gas Station
▬▬▬	Ferry	•	Accommodation	🕊	Waterfall	🐟	Dive Site
▬▬▬	Railroad	▼	Restaurant/Bar	▲	Park		Mangrove
▬▬▬	Pedestrian Walkway	■	Other Location	☐	Trailhead		Reef
▭▭▭	Stairs	▲	Campground	☩	Lighthouse		Swamp

CONVERSION TABLES

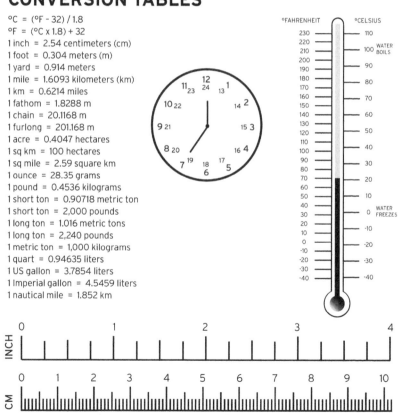

$°C = (°F - 32) / 1.8$

$°F = (°C \times 1.8) + 32$

1 inch = 2.54 centimeters (cm)
1 foot = 0.304 meters (m)
1 yard = 0.914 meters
1 mile = 1.6093 kilometers (km)
1 km = 0.6214 miles
1 fathom = 1.8288 m
1 chain = 20.1168 m
1 furlong = 201.168 m
1 acre = 0.4047 hectares
1 sq km = 100 hectares
1 sq mile = 2.59 square km
1 ounce = 28.35 grams
1 pound = 0.4536 kilograms
1 short ton = 0.90718 metric ton
1 short ton = 2,000 pounds
1 long ton = 1.016 metric tons
1 long ton = 2,240 pounds
1 metric ton = 1,000 kilograms
1 quart = 0.94635 liters
1 US gallon = 3.7854 liters
1 Imperial gallon = 4.5459 liters
1 nautical mile = 1.852 km

MOON SPOTLIGHT MEDELLÍN & COLOMBIA'S COFFEE REGION

Avalon Travel
a member of the Perseus Books Group
1700 Fourth Street
Berkeley, CA 94710, USA
www.moon.com

Editor: Leah Gordon
Series Manager: Kathryn Ettinger
Copy Editor: Deana Shields
Graphics and Production Coordinator: Domini Dragoone
Cover Design: Faceout Studios, Charles Brock
Moon Logo: Tim McGrath
Map Editor: Mike Morgenfeld
Cartographer: Stephanie Poulain

ISBN-13: 978-1-63121-099-0

ABOUT THE AUTHOR

Andrew Dier

Andrew Dier and his Colombian partner Vio arrived in Bogotá from New York City in 2002. It was initially supposed to be a temporary move – a change of scenery for a while – but 10 years and a couple of adopted street dogs later, bustling Bogotá has become their home.

Excited to share his insider perspective on Colombia with others, Andrew is continuously astounded by the natural beauty of the country and touched by the genuine warmth of its people.

Andrew is a regular contributor to *The City Paper*, an English-language newspaper in Bogotá, and has written for a number of publications in the United States. He's also become a deft translator, mostly for local nonprofit organizations.